PUNK
FICTION

PUNK
FICTION

Edited by
Janine Bullman

PORTICO

First published in the United Kingdom in 2009 by
Portico Books
10 Southcombe Street
London
W14 0RA

An imprint of Anova Books Company Ltd

ISBN 9781906032661

A CIP catalogue record for this book is available from the British Library.

10 9 8 7 6 5 4 3 2 1

Typeset by SX Composing DTP, Rayleigh, Essex
Printed and bound by CPI Mackays, Chatham, Kent, ME5 8TD

This book can be ordered direct from the publisher at anovabooks.com

Teenage Cancer Trust is a registered charity.
Charity Registration No. 1062559
Scottish Charity Reg. No. SC039757
www.teenagecancertrust.org

contents

Foreword	*Johnny Marr*	vii
Introduction	*Janine Bullman*	x
Gimme Danger	*Nicholas Hogg*	1
West One (Shine on Me)	*Joolz Denby*	14
Midget Submarines	*Max Décharné*	19
Cattle and Cane	*John Niven*	27
Shoplifting	*Kele Okereke*	32
Oliver's Army	*Martin Lloyd Edwards*	40
Psycho Killer	*Alison Mosshart*	48
California Über Alles	*Lane Ashfeldt*	58
Safety Pin In My Heart	*Janine Bullman*	67
Redondo Beach	*Krissi Murison*	74
Time's Up	*Laura Barton*	84
Sheena is a Punk Rocker	*Cathi Unsworth*	91
Another Girl, Another Planet	*Paul Smith*	109
Dancing Barefoot	*Lois Wilson*	116
Ever Fallen in Love	*Salena Godden*	121
Public Image	*Kate Pullinger*	130
Career Opportunities	*Lee Bullman*	136
Once in a Lifetime	*Alan Donohoe*	145
Liebe And Romanze	*Laura Oldfield Ford*	149
Fodderstompf	*Peter Wild*	161
Germ Free Adolescents	*Will Hodgkinson*	166
Get Yourself Killed	*Stewart Home*	176

The Day the World Turned		
Day-Glo	*Kate Jackson*	180
Anarchy in the UK	*Edward Larrikin*	192
Loco Mosquito	*Jay Clifton*	196
She is Beyond Good		
and Evil	*David Gaffney*	211
Shot By Both Sides	*Lydia Lunch*	218
The KKK Took		
My Baby Away	*Dev Hynes*	224
Revolution Rock	*Billy Bragg*	232
action time and vision	*Billy Childish*	240
Afterword: Spiral Scratch	*John Robb*	253

£1 from every copy of *Punk Fiction* sold will go to
Teenage Cancer Trust, a charity devoted
to improving the lives of teenagers and
young adults with cancer.

For more details on this charity, please go to
www.teenagecancertrust.org

Foreword by Johnny Marr

'Here's a chord, here's another, here's a third . . . now go and form a band'.

This was the seminal phrase and call to arms from the pages of punk rock's most important fanzine *Sniffin' Glue*. This simple handwritten instruction was the perfect illustration of the youth's new manifesto: discard the outdated establishment bullshit, go out and be creative, and never mind the bollocks.

The punk movement began as a covert reaction to the uninspired drabness of the UK's straight culture; it was sharp and funny and switched on. It was about excitement and subversion and being young. But mostly it was about new ideas.

The young and inspired put these new ideas out in an explosion of expression and creativity as they formed new kinds of bands, dressed in their own way (with their own new identities to match). They opened shops and clubs, creating an entirely new kind of lifestyle and aesthetic. Some of them became writers and journalists, some started their own fanzines, and some wrote lyrics.

So much has been said about punk's revolution in music and fashion that the story of its revolution via the printed word has been overlooked.

There had always been a huge aspect of punk

informed by literary culture; Television's Tom Verlaine and Richard Hell started out as young poets and essayists, with the former taking his name from the French symbolist poet and Hell taking his attitude and image (now credited as the invention of the punk look) from Arthur Rimbaud.

The band who are widely regarded as the first ever punk rock group got their name and greatest song from books – *The Velvet Underground* was a paperback by Michael Leigh and of course 'Venus in Furs' was inspired by Leopold Von Sacher-Masoch's book of the same name.

UK bands too looked on bookshelves for inspiration, with Generation X taking their name from a sixties paperback and the works of Guy Debor and the seminal Situationist International providing some much needed political rhetoric for Malcolm McLaren and The Clash.

The music press too, crucial in spreading the word to the soon-to-be-converted, had never before been more important as a new generation of writers engaged in ousting not only redundant bands but also the old guard of hacks who were responsible for putting those dull stars up in the cosmos in the first place. Every week claimed new blood, but most importantly it brought new creation, bringing with its words and pictures a new creed, new ways, and new stories.

There were stories about the Notting Hill riots, there were stories about Bored Teenagers and there were stories about Being Stranded. There were stories about Outdoor Miners and Germ Free Adolescents and Orgasm Addicts.

All punk was about a story. It was about living the story in your own head, good or bad. Whether that story was fact or fiction didn't matter, as long as it wasn't boring.

This book brings together stories with the punk spirit in the hope that they might inspire, provoke or simply entertain, as punk did: 'Here's a song, here's another, here's a third . . . now go and write a story.'

So it goes.

Introduction

Punk Fiction is a collection of short stories inspired by punk songs. The contributors – mainly writers and musicians – have been hand picked from the generations following the punk revolution; those who were positively influenced by the movement rather than those who played an active part in making it happen. Their instructions were simple: pick a punk song that inspires you and write. Nicholas Hogg chose Iggy Pop's 'Gimme Danger' because it reminded him of the recklessness of youth. Joolz Denby chose The Ruts' 'West One (Shine on Me)' because The Ruts played the best gig she'd ever been to.

There were no rules.

Some of the writers responded to the lyrics, some the title, others to what they perceived to be punk. Others listened to the song on repeat and were inspired by the emotions and images the music conjured. This freedom resulted in Edward Larrikin's 'Anarchy in the UK', written entirely in lowercase. It also allowed Billy Childish to write his story 'action, time and vision' in his own dyslexic style.

Punk Fiction is not about safety pins and mohicans. The idea was to bring together an eclectic mix of writers and musicians who *are* punk and mavericks in their own right. As the musician Paul Smith put it, 'Punk inspires other people to create, which is why I wanted to write something for this book.'

My aim was for the finished book to show that the

punk rock legacy was not merely musical, but that the stones it cast upon the surface of our culture made ripples which reached every corner of life and, to this day, continue to do so.

This book is for charity. This means all the writers wrote for free and wrote against impossible deadlines; initial conception to completion of the book took no less than five months. For some of the musicians it was their very first foray into short story writing and it was a very brave thing to do. So it is to all the writers that I would like to offer my most grateful thanks for their generosity, time and belief in the project – in particular to Lois Wilson for her unreserved support throughout.

The beneficiary of this book is Teenage Cancer Trust, a charity devoted to improving the lives of teenagers and young adults with cancer.

Janine Bullman
December 2008, London

In 1984 I was ten years old. The punks I knew from the park and brook represented a darker edge of my estate – glue sniffing under the bridge, hanging around the derelict factories in town. The brooding, threatening opening bars of Iggy Pop & The Stooges' 'Gimme Danger' set the atmosphere for what messing around with the older, reckless kids really felt like. I was too young for punk music, but my love at that age for smashing things up and setting fire to anything that would burn was something of a punk attitude.

Gimme Danger

Nicholas Hogg

Just before we set fire to him, Fish-head told me about his bullet necklace.

'They reckon,' he said, drawing the links up and over his T-shirt, 'that everyone in the world's got a bullet with their name on.'

And there it was, between his thumb and finger.

'See that?'

I looked closer. It really was a bullet. Silver. Engraved on the casing was his name.

'Terry Munton,' I read aloud.

'Fish-head's just me nickname,' he assured. 'No fucker's gonna shoot me with my bullet if it's hanging around me neck.'

But I'm getting ahead of myself. It was 1984, and like most of the kids on my estate I was break-dancing and body popping on strips of kitchen lino. Punk was dead. And those that survived had been pushed underground. Literally. The glue sniffers had the bridge, and we had the park.

I was a ten-year-old head-spin prince sharing Superkings with the older girls, and swigs of Scandia Green. We called our crew Atomic Rock. I'd begged my mum for a red and blue Nike jacket so I could troop the colours. No one else my age had one.

Until Stephan Bates came out of borstal.

'Why the fuck are you on my park?'

For two months I'd hung around the swings, moonwalked and windmilled.

'I'm asking you a question.' Batesy was fifteen. Not big, but an ancient giant when you're still at primary school. 'You hear me, you little fuck?'

I had a reputation as a bit of a pyro. True, I did like a good fire, but I wasn't the one who'd torched his old man's shed.

'I got caught nicking that mower because you wrecked his old one.'

Again, I said, 'It weren't me.'

He was having none of it. He took his dog off its lead, then lashed me with that fucking chain. The dog got excited, too, biting at the Nike jacket tied around my waist. I could hear some of the girls shouting, 'Pack it in, Steph.' But the dog snarled and snagged its teeth on the sleeves. I untied the coat and legged it down the railway cutting. Not until I was across the brook and over the fence into the building site did I stop running.

But, bollocks. I was supposed to be home once the streetlights came on, and the bulbs already buzzed. No chance of going back across the park, and I'd be well late if I had to walk all the way up College Road.

Fuck it. I had no choice but to sneak along the edge of the brook and under the bridge.

Past the punks.

I followed a dirt path that cut between the water and the park. It was getting dark, tree branches turned to silhouettes on the technicolour dusk, a night sky decorated no doubt by fumes from the paint factories in town. Before I got to the bridge I could smell something burning, fags. And I could hear a tinny stereo distorting. Before the end of the path I stopped and spied through the bushes.

Sitting around a fire of pallet wood nicked from the building site, drinking beer from plastic bottles, dressed in black and pierced with silver, sat the punks. They looked like some cave tribe cooking up their kill.

I waited and watched. They passed around a carrier bag, inhaled, exhaled, puffed it up like a polythene lung. The only one not in leather wore an army jacket. This was Fish-head. He poked the fire with a steel rod, then pulled it out glowing, jabbing it towards a skinny kid flat on his back.

I thought this might be a good chance to sneak past. I was nearly in the water; then I slipped and I *was* in the water. The splash echoed under the bridge.

'What we got here, then?'

Wet feet or not, I carried on walking through the shallows.

'Hold on, little man.' It was Fish-head, the one with the steel rod, a crucifix inked below his left eye. 'What's the rush?'

I wasn't past them yet, and I thought running might make me look like something to be chased, so I stopped. 'Just going home.'

'Do you live in the fucking brook?' This made them laugh. 'And what the fuck are you doing in just a T-shirt? It's freezing.'

I got out of the water, but stayed at the bottom of the bank. 'I lost me coat.'

'How do you lose a coat?'

'Well, a dog nicked it.' This had them pissing themselves laughing. The roars rattled back and forth across the brook, waking the skinny kid laid out on the concrete. He sat up, then leapt up, screaming, 'Fuck. Fuck. Me fucking feet are burning.'

He'd crashed out with his boots in the fire, and now he came jumping down the bank and into the water, stomping, dancing in the brook.

Fish-head shouted, 'Pogo it, Raggy.'

Raggy flipped out, kicked up water and thrashed. The others loved him, screaming, cheering his flailing limbs. And when he finally slipped and fell, I was already wet, so it was no bother to help him.

'Little man,' called Fish-head. 'Push the daft fucker up here.'

Raggy, the 'daft fucker', was all over the place. I had his elbow and shoved him toward the fire. He collapsed onto the lap of a girl with a chain from her nose to her ear. I turned to go when Fish-head said, 'Hold up, mate.' He kicked Raggy. 'Thank him. You could've fucking drowned.'

'He can have me chips.' The girl with the chain passed me the greasy bag.

'Cheers.' I took a soggy handful.

They watched me eat. The crappy stereo bounced with a *bam, bam, bam, bam*. A man sang as if it would save his life. Or kill him. I ate the chips and asked what music was playing.

'You ain't heard of The Stooges?'

I hadn't.

'That scream belongs to the granddaddy of punk.'

A girl across the fire said, 'Little man's a breakdancer, ain't you?'

'Gymspastics,' said Raggy. 'That's what it is.'

'Ain't our voice,' added Fish-head. 'That's for fucking sure.'

'I ain't in their stupid crew anymore.'

'Well fuck 'em, little man, that's what I say. Kitchen lino is for kitchen floors. And dancing? Raggy's the dance master.'

'Pogo King.'

'Believe it.'

Flames wobbled. Other faces around the fire hung like masks. Painted faces, girls with purple lipstick. I was quite happy standing there finishing off Raggy's chips, but I could see the streetlights reflected in the brook, the black water rippled with amber. I told them I had to go.

'Take it easy, little man.' That's what Fish-head said. And when he did I realised that usually the break-dancing crew said fuck all when I left.

I was grounded for a week. Whacked three or four times by my stepdad because I ducked his first swing and pissed him right off. A fucking week sat in my crummy little bedroom. And no TV. And fucked if I was listening to Electro 7 if I was kicked out the crew. I twisted the radio dial to see if I could find something like that Stooges I heard under the bridge. But all I got was Madonna and Billy Ocean.

My first day back out I rode straight up the park. I could see Dave Hillman's Escort. I could hear the break beats pulsing from his bass buckets.

Then I swear Batesy's dog saw me before Batesy did. He held that mutt by its collar and pointed and shook it around till it got so angry it could do nothing but chase me.

I was already pedalling when he set it loose. Fuck that dog. I should count myself lucky it didn't shred my skin last time and just got my sleeves. The sleeves of a uniform I could no longer wear.

I caned it round Jez Stevens'. As I'd been banged up for a week, I soon got bored in his house. We put Ghostbusters on his Spectrum and waited for what seemed about two years before it loaded. I was glad when his old man came home from work and said it was time for Jez's lunch.

So I rode over to the bridge. It was a Saturday afternoon, a sunny one for late autumn. I stashed my bike under the bushes. Condoms and aerosol cans littered the path to the water. I admit I was a bit nervous. Once you were down there, you were right into whatever was happening. I'd seen couples with jeans around their ankles, two kids from the travellers' site cutting open a rabbit, a tramp shitting in the water.

Only there was no one about today. Just a burnt out TV, plastic bags, graffiti daubed on concrete: *No Future, Open Up and Bleed, Anarchy in the UK*, and always talk about someone sucking someone else's cock.

I slid down the bank of rocks stuck together with cement. The water was usually brown, like tea before you put the milk in. I was turning over broken paving slabs looking for frogs when someone lobbed a brick past my shoulder.

'Bastard, watch it.'

I turned around. Raggy was grinning, his mohican stood freshly spiked. 'Missed you by miles.' He looked on the same empty wreckage I had minutes before. 'You seen Fish-head?'

'I ain't seen no one.'

'Bollocks.' He just stood, scratched at his forehead till it turned scarlet. Then he asked if I had 50p.

'I don't even get pocket money.'

'Hard life, innit?' He kicked a stone into the water. 'That your Grifter in the bushes?'

I didn't want to say it was, because I guessed he had to get somewhere and it involved my wheels.

'Lend us it for ten minutes.'

'You ain't nicking me bike.'

He looked at me then turned back to the path. I ran up the bank behind him. By the time I got to the top he was standing my bike up.

'Fuck off.' I grabbed the handlebars. 'Me stepdad'll batter you if he sees you riding it.'

He thought about that. I saw the spots around his mouth and nose. 'Well I'll give you a croggy into town.'

It was either that, home, or lifting up stones under the bridge.

I stood on the wheel nuts and held Raggy's leather jacket. We took the path round the back of the Co-op, just in case my little brother saw us and grassed me up. Not that I was doing anything wrong.

Yet.

Raggy rode us to the derelict factory on Broad Street. Since it had shut down the council had come and fenced it off. A pointless task in a town with fuck all to do but break in to places just like that. We went through a gap in the mesh and Raggy laid the bike in a patch of stinging nettles. 'No fucker's nicking it out of that.'

'I'll get stung myself.'

'Don't be a ponce.'

I watched him walk over to the metal fire escape. The barbed wire, once twisted around the bottom rungs, had been ripped off. Raggy started climbing. When he saw I wasn't following he looked down. 'You scared or something?'

'No. I've been in before, anyway.'

Only a few weeks ago me and Jez had climbed the very same fire escape and crawled in through the broken window. But when we heard someone moving around in one of the offices we'd more or less shit ourselves and run.

This time I was going in and staying. Raggy was right, I was a bit scared, but it was better than being bored.

Or sitting at home waiting to piss my stepdad off.

Or standing around the edge of a gang who didn't even know I was there.

I followed the soles of his Doc Martens through that window. He grabbed my jacket so I didn't hit the glass on the floor.

'You meeting Fish-head?'

'I hope so.'

What they once made in that factory I have no idea. A balcony of offices looked down onto some kind of machine shop. Hulks of metal, cogs and wheels and levers that once whirred and turned, now rusted away.

'Spooky as fuck,' said Raggy, looking about the factory. A couple of pigeons fluttered around a skylight. Then he said, 'Fuck this,' and shouted, 'Fish-head, you cunt.'

No answer, just the flapping pigeons.

'Come on.' He walked around the balcony and down a corridor with offices along each side.

It was another point I could've turned around.

I didn't. I took two more steps when a fucking boot came through one of the plasterboard walls. Raggy leapt back, grabbing me as he did. Another boot appeared. It was like a horror film. The dead had come back to life and were kicking their way out of the grave.

Luckily, the dead were dressed in camo jackets.

'Fucking hell, Fish-head.'

Fish-head stuck his wide face through one of the holes. Manic, smiling, teeth missing. 'Shit you up, did I?' Then he shrank back and kicked and smashed his way into the corridor, laughing, dusted with Gypsum. Fish-head was in hysterics, and only when he got his breath back did he say, 'Little man, I knew you had some punk in you.'

Raggy slapped Fish-head on the shoulder. 'You're a proper cunt.'

I followed them past ransacked offices littered with sheets of accounts and letters from people who no longer had those jobs. All the drawers had been yanked from the desks. You might think an invading army had been through and pillaged, that each room was the scene of some terrible crime, and perhaps some were, but mostly all that had happened was that kids, like us, had found them.

In the end room was a table. On the table were rolls of paper caps for toy guns, Sellotape and gravel.

'You know how to make throwing bangers?'

I told Fish-head that of course I did. 'What you gonna do with 'em?'

'We make ten each, then run around the factory lobbing 'em at each other.'

'It's a right laugh,' confirmed Raggy.

So we sat about that table like good students in an

art class. First we folded the strips of caps lengthways, so the gunpowder spilt out, then twisted the paper around the gravel before taping it into a ball. Once thrown they were live, going bang when they hit something and the stones sparked the charge.

While we worked Fish-head explained that being a punk wasn't just about liking the music. 'Or what you wear. It's about attitude. You gotta have the "fuck you" approach to life.'

Raggy looked at my trainers. 'I know it ain't about clothes, but we gotta get you some proper shoes.'

I was wearing my Hi-Tec Silver Shadows.

'Para boots.' Fish-head whacked his size tens on the table. 'But make sure you pull the German's toes out first.'

That was when he showed me the necklace with the bullet, the one with his name on.

That was just before we heard a door being smashed in from the floor below.

'Shit,' said Raggy. 'Coppers?'

'Hold on,' ordered Fish-head. He tilted his head and listened. We all did. And I was scared. I wasn't even eleven, and I wondered what my step dad would do to me if I went home in a police car.

But whatever the danger was, it was a fucking rush.

When the whining revs of a 50cc bike reverberated around that empty factory, Fish-head said, 'No pig rides a chip shop racer. Get the bangers.'

We filled our pockets and crept along the corridor. Fish-head got to the balcony and crouched. Someone was thrashing the fuck out of that bike. Once Fish-head had stood and cocked his arm to throw, me and Raggy took aim. From the balcony the kid looked like a figure on a wind-up stunt bike, a child's toy let rip. He did a circuit, zipping slaloms between the machines. On the straight towards us Fish-head threw, so did Raggy. And so did I. He was riding into a war zone. The bangers flashed and cracked, and it might have been my throw, I'm not sure, but the one that bounced off his shoulder dropped him. Bike and rider skittered along the concrete and slammed into the end wall.

'Fucking shit,' exclaimed Raggy.

'Bollocks,' added Fish-head.

It was when he started wriggling we could see he must be all right.

And it was then I realised that it was Stephan Bates.

I think his tracky bottoms were snagged on the bike, and he was trying to yank them free. Much the same way I tried to get away from his dog when it had my jacket.

And perhaps it was with this thought that I threw.

I missed Batesy and his bike. But I hit a petrol spill from the tank. Though there was no Hollywood explosion, the fire quickly flared around the back wheel. Batesy found he could wriggle himself free after all, frantic, running from the factory with his coat sleeve smouldering. No, not *his*, the sleeve of *my* fucking coat.

We ran, too. Fish-head dragged me down those fire escape steps and over the fence and across the car park of the new industrial estate. And we didn't stop running till we got to the train yard. Raggy helped me up onto one of the old carriages so we could see the factory, the smoke, then the fire engines.

'Fucking hell, man,' he said. 'They've even got the one with the crane.'

We could see a man aiming a hose from the top of a ladder. Fish-head slapped my back. 'Don't give a fuck, do you?'

I said I didn't. Though I was bothered about my Grifter, but I guessed I could pull it from the stingers later.

We watched the factory burn. You could hear glass splitting with the heat, see flames bursting from the windows.

I knew I'd have to deal with Batesy again at some point, but I also knew I might have some help next time, because Fish-head asked me what my name was and promised to engrave it onto a bullet.

To me, The Ruts always embodied the true, eclectic, questioning, honest nature of punk: 'West One (Shine on Me)' is a brilliantly fearless composition with tremendous build, touching on the sad, savage nature of youthful disillusion with the world and the truly romantic feel of a young voice crying out in the night for justice. It never fails to move me, to energise me and to make me remember what it was to be young.

West One (Shine on Me)

Joolz Denby

It was 1979, not that I remembered because to be honest I am totally shit with dates. Anyway, it was cold as witch-breath, I can tell you that, and the pub looked like one of those cheap faux-Dickensian Christmas cards, eggnog yellow light streaming out onto Manningham Lane's unreeling strip of car-pocked grey.

What night of the week was it? Don't know. Don't remember much about the details really. I never was one of those obsessive fans who know every note played, every set-list, every T-shirt bought and the names of the bass player's cats (the third bass player, that is, the one after Nobby and before Charlie, the one who – oh, you know the type of true believer, the one who writes you letters in biro on paper torn out of a cheap notebook asking for the tab for the second song on your first demo that you thought no one but you had a copy of).

I only know it was 1979 because I looked it up on the internet. The Ruts, Bradford, The Royal Standard, 1979. That was weird in itself, looking up a gig you went to 31 years ago, thinking about it, remembering what you were wearing, what colour your hair was dyed, who was with you. Who's still alive. Whose head is fucked from drugs and alcohol. Who's still OK, still hanging in there, still making stuff. Remembering being young. Looking in the mirror and thinking – who's that old woman? And behind the reflection, the ghost of a big, furious, scarlet-haired girl with a thousand-yard stare, dancing, dancing.

So I trawled the internet looking for the lost past. Not that there was much information out there, oddly. But then, why would I think it odd? An obscure gig by an obscure band in an obscure city. I feel that way because it was, without doubt, one of the greatest rock concerts ever played – and remember, I'm not that obsessive fan. I'm someone who's toiled in the dark, grubby bowels of the music industry for thirty years.

I've seen more bands than most people have had hot dinners or rolled a half-decent blunt. I've seen bands big, small and hyped-to-fuck. In bars, clubs, pubs, concert halls and festivals. Every type of rock band possible, every permutation of sweaty-boy-yodelling-into-mic. Some yodelling girls, but trust me, not many. I have seen and compared them to that gig. Ninety-nine percent of them didn't even get near to measuring up to that show, and wouldn't even know how to try.

I did find out The Ruts are now claimed by the gormless, beer-bellied banga-banga fuckwits who claim to be punk these days. The sad fifty-year-olds with the thinning blue mohican instead of a comb-over, the painted leather jacket, emblazoned with Anarchy signs, sagging with nickel studs, and the pint clutched like a child's comforter. The impervious young glue-heads desperate to find a moral oblivion whose rigid sartorial and musical dictates protect them from the cruelty of growing up. The lowest common denominator, the ones we dandy punk gentry with our self-righteous pretensions to world revolution and the esoteric fibrillations of justice, fairness and a better society, called Oi Punks – Gary Bushell's Frankenstein's monster. If the *Sun* invents a youth movement, surely it would be better to hurl yourself ablaze from the White Cliffs of Dover than, like, join it?

But in 1979, The Ruts were an up-and-coming outfit from London, daring to break through the wall of mist that descends after Watford Gap, when the tarmac turns to cobbles, the sound of wild ferrets howling fills queasy Southern ears and the motorway signs just say, The North. The Ruts were playing The Royal Standard, a dog-rough boozer on the Lane with a mighty concert room attached to it that regularly saw the finest punk bands the world had to offer struggling to understand the landlord's strange obsession with bands nicking cheese from his fridge and his impenetrable Clayton accent. The Ruts were, we thought, just another gig.

I don't know. Was it the room? The sound? (Couldn't have been, it was always arse). The fact the place was packed out? The contrast between the iron-cold Bradford winter outside and the heat of a hundred punks inside? The light? It seemed golden, effervescent – but that couldn't be true. Or were the planets in the right alignment? Mars bang overhead and the North Star shining on us all, blessing us, cursing us.

Whatever, it's all a blaze of fire in my head, in my memory; untarnished, unalloyed, pure. Malcolm Owen sings, possessed, entranced, without reservation, not worrying if he's cool or on message, or if the marketing department approve, none of that old tosh, he just sings with an awful clarity that burns us all up, that re-arranges the molecular structure of our hearts forever, that binds us to a purpose we have never abandoned. It was like being in the eye of a hurricane, in a cauldron boiling with energy and a kind of infectious epiphany. Outside the world could have vanished into Hell and nothingness, but in that shitty, murder-haunted, perfect box we were all warriors, shield-maidens, purified. None of us left unmarked by that experience and some of us were changed forever; some of us saw what we could aim for, what we could be, what we could break our hearts trying for. What we still try for.

Less than a year later, Malcolm Owen was dead from a heroin overdose; his struggle with himself over. He was 26. Just 26.

Before he died, he and The Ruts had recorded 'West One (Shine on Me)'. It was released in 1980. In it there's a line, 'Bradford shine on me.'

He knew what that gig was, too.

I picked 'Midget Submarines' firstly because it's such a great song. The Swell Maps were everything that punk was supposed to be about – do-it-yourself, loads of imagination, genuinely uplifting. I met Nikki Sudden from the Maps in the mid-80s and wound up playing drums and piano with him on numerous occasions over the next twenty years. He and his brother Epic are both gone now – here's to them.

Midget Submarines

Max Décharné

Part One – A Trip to Marineville

Danny stared out into the darkness as the carriage rattled across the railway bridge into Pompey, leaving behind the motorway underpass with its foot-high scrawled message: MILLWALL DON'T COME IN.

That warning wasn't meant for the likes of him, but he was wary, just the same. Ripped white shirt, safety pins, straight jeans, hacked-up school tie, cropped spiky hair and a scattering of badges – short of hanging a neon sign around his neck saying, 'Please beat the fuck out of me', he couldn't have done much more to wind up the local after-pub philosophers. Christ, just the fact that you didn't have flared trousers or shoulder-length hair was enough to start the alarm bells ringing.

Black oily water down below, and the distant lights of the harbour off to the right, where the rusting, decommissioned hulks of wartime submarines were lined up on the mudbanks, chained together as if someone was worried they might make a break for it. Maybe it was just that anything that wasn't nailed down would be knocked off in the middle of the night and flogged by some enterprising young fucker who'd unaccountably missed his chance of a place on the Duke of Edinburgh's Award scheme.

The school had taken Danny and his class on a trip round the dockyard once, piled into a small boat on a fearsomely cold day for a close-up view of half a century's worth of surplus naval hardware slowly rotting away. His teacher said that the navy's first ever submariners had slithered around under these waters back in 1901, poor bastards. Would they have been in a midget submarine? Hard to say, but he'd had this tune running round in his head ever since he'd taped that Peel Session by the Swell Maps the previous week: a raw, repetitive song with a hell of a chorus, that repeated the words 'midget submarine . . . midget submarine . . .' over and over. Fuck knows what they were on about, but it drilled itself into your brain and it sounded exactly right: you could just tell that these people knew what they were doing, and had a sense of humour about it into the bargain.

Peel was the only one turning up stuff like that. Danny listened to the show most week nights from ten till midnight with his radio cassette machine, fingers on the buttons ready to tape the beginning of each tune. Hit 'play' and 'record' just as John was announcing the name of the song, then let it roll and see how he liked it. If it didn't make an impression after thirty seconds or so, then he'd wind the tape back and cue it up at the end of the previous recording, and be ready in time for the introduction to the next song. By Saturday each week, he'd have enough stuff on tape which had made the grade, and would head for HMV in Pompey to try to buy the best of what he'd heard. No question, Danny would have bought the lot if he could have afforded it. 'Midget Submarines' wasn't a single, though, so he would have to wait for the album Peel had said would be out in about a month. Right now, he had that song going round in his head on constant repeat as the train finally crawled past the coal yards by Fratton Park.

Part Two – Vertical Slum

Danny checked the gig ticket in his pocket one more time – *The Jam + The Vapours, £3.50, Portsmouth Guildhall, 7.30*. Just coming up to 8.45. With luck he'd have missed the support group, and would hit the hall just in time for Weller and his crew. Last time he'd seen The Jam there'd been no question whatever that they were a punk band. He'd been on holiday with his family down in the West Country, read in the *NME* that the group were playing at Torquay Town Hall, and caught them doing a blistering set in front of a solid mass of spiky-haired kids from the blank generation. That was about two years previously, though. Since then, the rules had changed. The whole toy mod revival had swept through the kids three or four years younger than him, and it seemed like every other fourteen-year-old in town was wearing a freshly-bought fishtail parka with a target painted on the back. Fair enough, mate, thought Danny, a riot of yer own, but this was our band before you'd ever heard of them.

He swung open the carriage door and stepped out onto the overhead platform at Pompey & Southsea station. Tonight's show was at the Guildhall, which was lucky – only a few hundred yards to walk, and there'd be a fair old crowd for it, so the chances of being hassled by the local meatheads were somewhat reduced. Not like '77. First punk band he'd seen in town was X-Ray Spex, just when 'Oh Bondage Up Yours' came out. Some joker had booked them into a place called the Oddfellows Hall, after a whole summer of the tabloids telling every fucker that punks cut up dead babies for a laugh and spit on pictures of the Queen, gawd bless 'er, and if you see one in the street, then give them hell. The advert in the Pompey *Evening News* – '*Exciting London Beat Combo X-Ray Spex, 75p*' – had made the severe tactical mistake of listing not only the start, but also the *finish* time of the gig. This meant that when the fifty or so teenagers who'd watched Polly and her gang do the business with the aid of the world's cheapest PA system finally emerged from the building, half the Teddy Boys in town were waiting across the street, ready to have a go at these snotty young upstarts. Running like hell, ducking down side streets, hiding in among the damp, useless boarded-up shop units of Britain's least-favourite building, the Tricorn Centre – anywhere to get away from the punk-bashing vigilantes. Yeah, they'd all had a bit of exercise that evening.

Somewhere along the line, though, punk had become almost a mainstream taste. The likes of The Stranglers had been on *Top of the Pops* doing 'Go Buddy Go', and when The Clash hit Pompey on the *Sort it Out* tour at the end of '78 to play the Locarno, all the local punks had turned out in force. Danny had been shocked to see how many people like him there were, snaking down the street in a long line maybe seven or eight hundred strong as the promoters failed to open the doors anywhere near the advertised time. Prior to that, you'd be lucky to run into a handful of geezers in ripped-up, hand-stencilled Oxfam clothing anywhere you went in Pompey. Long hair, and tank tops were the fashion, and *Saturday Night* fucking *Fever* was the real sound of '77, here and most other places, and the few punks on the streets were outnumbered pretty much everywhere they went. In among the high-rise, low-rent rubbish that had been built to cover the vast areas of wartime bomb damage around town, you kept your eyes open and your head down. Danny could have done with a bloody midget submarine just to escape sometimes.

Part Three – Real Shocks

11.00pm, piling out of the venue, ears still ringing, half the crowd looked barely old enough to tie their own shoelaces, but maybe the mods had a point – this wasn't really a punk band anymore. Still, the band had done 'Down In The Tube Station', and that new one, 'Strange Town', so Danny was happy – both of them nice little paranoid outsider songs about London from someone who lived a little further down the railway line that led into Waterloo. Danny could identify with that. A Woking-class hero is something to be . . .

Danny ducked a little way down Commercial Road, taking a chance on finding a chippie that was still open before braving the train journey home. Funnily enough, even with a shedload of Jam numbers still fresh in his mind, the song that kept coming back to him was that Maps one from the Peel session, 'Midget Submarines'. He'd played it to death the past week, but still didn't know any more of the words than just the title, but that's all you needed – that and the insistent guitar line running round your head. The band were from Birmingham, or somewhere nearby, and had funny names. Mind you, everyone and his wife on the punk scene had a made-up name, but these were better than most: Epic Soundtracks, Biggles Books, Jowe Head Nikki Sudden. Just from those, you could tell they had the right attitude.

It looked like luck was on Danny's side. Here was a chippie and, apart from an older bloke in one of those tatty khaki flasher macs, there was no one in there. Thirty pence-worth of chips, money on the counter, and out sharpish hoping he hadn't missed his last train. Danny ran round the corner to the station, up to the platform and into a carriage right near the back just a minute before the train pulled away. There'd been a couple of stragglers from the gig crowd still hanging about, but mostly they'd gone – probably picked up by mummy and daddy in a posh car, complaining that it was way past their bedtime. What the hell. Danny had some chips, and he stared up at the scratched-up warning notice above the carriage door, which had been altered, like all the others he'd ever seen, to read 'Do Not Clean Soup Off The Window'.

A few people got on at Fratton, but no one much to worry about, and the train headed out through the south of Portsea Island, past the looming towers of Hilsea Gasworks, grinding to a stop at Hilsea Halt – a short strip of platform where hardly anyone ever got on or off. Tonight, though, someone did.

There were four of them. Big fuckers. Three of them sat opposite Danny and one right next to him. Right away the nearest one leaned over and started nicking his chips.

'What the bloody hell have we got here then? Fucking punk rock nancy boy is it? Where's the safety pin in your fucking *nose*?'

'His hair ain't spiky enough, is it. Lemme help you with that . . . '

The remaining contents of the chip packet were smeared all over his head, then a boot connected with his jaw, followed by several others, and the world went dark.

Part Four – Ripped & Torn

The nurse told him later that they'd found him in the mud, on the Cosham side of the railway bridge. Thrown from the train. Broken jaw, broken arm, concussion. All things considered, quite lucky really, she reckoned. Guess she had a point. Last thing he could remember was someone shouting, 'We're gonna spread your face all over Drayton.' Nice lads.

'What were you trying to do?' she asked, smiling. 'Swim home?'

'Nah,' mumbled Danny through his wired jaw. 'Better than that. Got a midget submarine . . .'

I've always been an enormous fan of The Go-Betweens, but death sharpens and personalises the lyrics of a pop song like nothing else. Apart from love.

Cattle and Cane

John Niven

In the hours and days after he died I tried to find a soundtrack to help me grieve.

I was staying at my girlfriend's flat in King's Cross the night the phone rang – small hours, December – and I rifled through the record collection for something suitable to mark his passing. For some unknowable reason her flatmate had an ancient Stiff Little Fingers compilation. There was a connection there.

When he was a teenager he'd had a stab at writing a few punk rock anthems of his own. One of them told the story of a young lad who rashly joined the army. In part its lyric ran: 'swapped civilian clothes for army ones' It was basically a (very) thin rewrite of the song 'Tin Soldiers' by Stiff Little Fingers. (Another of his songs, inspired by John Carpenter's *Assault on Precinct 13*, featured the unforgettable couplet: 'Goodies on the inside, baddies on the outside. It's a classic confrontation, between good and evil.')

I put 'Tin Soldiers' on for the first time in over twenty years, listening on headphones as I looked through the frosty window towards the cries and lights of King's Cross Station at the end of the road. My location that night was apposite: King's Cross was – had been – his kind of place. It was cold and I huddled under the duvet as I listened, trying to forge a connection between the circumstances and the music of our youth, but it wouldn't come, and neither would the tears, and after a while I turned the stereo off and went back to sleep.

Later, flying home to bury him, on the plane with the Discman, the peanuts and the Bloody Mary, I tried again to find a track that would work. We'd heard some details in the past week or so; talk of drugs and drink and checking into a Glasgow hotel on his own. I pressed my forehead against the freezing Perspex. Outside – deep and dark winter as we flew north, English skies silently becoming Scottish. I had a wallet of CDs on my lap and I flipped through the milky plastic sleeves, trying different songs, and still I could not cry.

At the funeral, back with all the boys, the people I had grown up with. We were all into our thirties now, heading towards middle age. Except for him, up there at the top of the church, headed nowhere, headed for the cold ground at the cemetery.

The music was good in the church. We all grew up music crazy. Kurt Cobain said he had been 'so alone' in his teens, growing up a punk rock obsessive in a small town. We were never like that – we all had each other, a tight group of outsiders for whom the 80s didn't mean Culture Club and Bezique and Del Boy. And now one of us was gone. We sat on hard benches and listened to Joy Division. To Gram Parsons singing 'n My Hour of Darkness'. Then a song I hadn't heard in many years; a rippling guitar riff, sparse and nimble, dreamy yet desolate. 'Cattle and Cane' by The Go-Betweens, Grant McLennan's tremulous eulogy for a childhood lived on the edge of Queensland, on the edge of the world. Weak sunlight lit the stained glass and the words echoed around the stone space:

> 'I recall, a schoolboy coming home,
> Through fields of cane,
> To a house of tin and timber
> And in the sky
> A rain of falling cinders.'

And I recalled my friend when he was a schoolboy. With a goofy grin and a bog-brush haircut and an infectious cackle. When he was a schoolboy coming home, not through beige clouds of outback dust, but through fields of heather and gorse, across the Scottish moors that ran opposite his house, and I wasn't really sure if he would have come home that way, but I was picturing it anyway and now Australia and Scotland and childhood were all bleeding together in my head and finally I was crying, my shoulders shaking and tears streaming down my face. I hunched over in the pew and wept as I thought about the boy I knew and about the young man he became.

And the old man he would never be.

The last words of the song are 'further, longer, higher, older'. But for him there was no further to go. No longer. No higher. No older.

Those who die much too young are freeze-framed at exactly the point we most wish to remember them. In my freeze-frame he is sitting on a low sofa in his attic bedroom. He is wearing a red canvas jacket with many zips. He has one leg crossed over the other so that the heel of his left Doc Marten boot rests on his right knee. He is balancing a mug of tea on the heel of the boot. In his other hand a cigarette is clutched in his own strange fashion, in a way I have never seen anyone else smoke a cigarette – clamped tightly between thumb and index finger about halfway along the tube, rather than by the filter. His head is thrown back, his mouth is open, his eyes are crinkled shut and he is laughing hard at something.

He is seventeen years old.

And outside the church, no rain of falling cinders. Just winter skies, as grey and cold and hard as Ayrshire.

In memoriam Larry Rhodes, 1967 – 2002

The Slits are probably my favourite punk group of all time, and there was a period when shoplifting was one of my favourite activities of all time . . . so picking 'Shoplifting' by The Slits to loosely base my first ever short story on was a bit of a no brainer.

Shoplifting

Kele Okereke

And all at once it came back to me, like the first crack
in a frozen lake, a sudden tightness in my chest, a
sensation I had not felt for such a long time. But it's
here now, for sure, exhilaration, pure liquid exhilaration. I am suddenly conscious of every movement
and contour of my tongue, every last pore. My mouth
is arid like a desert, chalky and coarse. And I am
glowing, I am sure that I am glowing, giving off an
invisible heat like a thousand fairy lights on the surface
of my skin. This is the feeling of the past being
rewritten, of everything I thought I knew being erased,
the endless possibilities of a new future.

I am trying to remember what I was thinking
when I woke this morning, but I can't. I know this
will sound trite but I knew today was going to
be different. There was something loose in the
November air; like the final piece of the puzzle had
fallen into place. Complicity. The morning alarm was
the same, roughly snatching me from the land of
dreams at 7.15 on the dot. The radio was the same,
playing that fuzz that they call music nowadays. The
shower, the cereal, the bus ride to the station, all the
same. But me, I was different. There was lightness,
where previously there had been none; the familiar
morning anxiety had evaporated. Could they see it

on my face on the train to work? Could they see it in the boardroom?

I have learnt from experience not to talk about my feelings. It brings discomfort to everyone involved, picking every scab, pulling everything apart. And also it's a reminder, a cruel reminder of the distance between me and everyone else. This 'bad habit' of mine has killed one too many gatherings, bored one too many new acquaintances. Strangers avoid me at parties and I don't blame them.

I remember when Melissa and I were driving to the Isle of Wight and she slammed her fists down on the steering wheel so hard that she bruised the side of her palms. The bruise lasted the whole week we were supposed to stay, a subtle remembrance charm, in purple and ochre. She said that I was being, 'unfair, self-obsessed and cruel', that she couldn't take this teenage bullshit anymore. If there was something in my life making me unhappy, I had to change it or just stop talking about it.

I had never seen this side of her before, not in conversation, or argument, or sex. She was always so placid, so calm, so matter of fact. This is what I loved about her from the start, her detachment. Isn't it funny that the things you first love in someone are often the things you grow to despise in the end? I remember that holiday so well, the stony silence afterwards in the car, the dread at what this coming week was going to bring. It was during this week that I realised that the function of avoidance is one of the most important in modern relationships. Only by pretending that this situation had never happened were we able to have any semblance of a good time.

I have this constant need to please and I don't

know where it comes from. Actually yes, yes I do, I know exactly where it comes from. It comes from my father. He always let my mother get what she wanted, he never put up a fight. Anything for a quiet life. He was so scared of losing her and rightly so. She was an atom bomb to his monotone grey. One of my earliest memories is of my mother chastising him in her famously cruel way. It was my eighth birthday and we had rented the community hall on top of the church. We had invited all my school friends and family, it was supposed to be a special day and it was, but for all the wrong reasons. All I can remember about this particular admonishment was that it had something to do with a Victoria sponge, but it was the look on my father's face that will stay with me for all time. There was something so unsettling about his composure, like he thought he deserved to be punished, that whatever slight error he made was on a par with committing a war crime and he knew it. She had the amazing knack of making him punish himself for what he had done and rather than focusing his anger externally he'd internalise it all. And in the end all of his fears came true, she left for Australia with one of his work colleagues. He was never the same man again and now I see so much of myself in him that it scares me . . . in how we both walk, in how we talk and how we respond to danger. We both think too much about the pointless things. Action is always something that has eluded us. Is history repeating itself?

School came easy to me, and it is not a conceit, it's true. It is all so logical, like Pythagoras' theorem. You apply the rules and see the results. There is almost no need for actual engagement and I'm pretty good at following rules. Don't get me wrong; in some respects

I was lucky. The bad boys and the troublemakers, they would always tell me how smart I was and me, I would let them copy my papers. I didn't mind. In fact I enjoyed it. I craved their attention. They envied me and I envied them. With their loose ties, their swagger and their recklessness. I wanted it, I wanted it so badly, but I just couldn't. Bound up in some silly code, I could never let myself cross the line. I think about them sometimes, and what they might be doing now. Selling plasma TVs? Cars? Drugs? And I am envious still. I always saw this 'gift' for what it was, a curse not a blessing. Such a powerful impulse, this need to please, to not stand out, to not let my parents down, to maintain. It can carry you through your teenage years, but what then? What about when the guidance stops, and the training wheels come off? And then it's up to you to work out what your life is going to mean.

Then there was university. All that talk of sexual abandonment, camaraderie, well that was just that, talk. While most people were casting off their inhibitions in a spectacular fashion (I could hear them most nights, copulating in their dorms and vomiting on the pavement at three in the morning) university life for me was a much more sedate affair. Nothing changed for me. I was wrapped up in my room, memorising Sartre, joylessly masturbating and listening to Pink Floyd. There was desire and the occasional embarrassing, alcohol-induced fumble, but I'm no Lothario. To be so wanton you would have to actually be a lover of life, you would have to see beauty somewhere, and that's not a capacity I ever had. No, my desire has always been a little too Church of England, a little too polite. I see it when I kiss her sometimes and I can tell when I look at her and she looks away that she can feel it too, the uncertainty, the rigidity of loveless repetition. I lay awake sometimes wondering what she could possibly see behind these eyes. How could she be so lost that she sees salvation in me?

There is a whole lot of loathing here, isn't there? I know I promised I wouldn't talk about my feelings, but I am trying to join the dots. Give you a little background as to who I was before today. I mean, it must have taken no more than sixty seconds, a minute and a half at a push. It seems that is all the time you need for a life to change. Before I go any further I must state clearly that what you are about to read was not premeditated. There was no suggestion or preamble, just instinct, motivated by a primal force.

Standing in the off licence, the planets aligned. Instinct became action, thought became motion.

The Bengali shopkeeper doesn't even look at me. Lost in some heated exchange on the phone, he carries on as if he hasn't even registered this quiet young businessman. I am nothing more than a mild irritation. And all the while, hugged to my core is the secret of my transgression pressed to my chest under the fold of my arm, inside my green Barbour jacket, condensation dampening my work shirt, a dull icy blast creeping out from under my arm, a trickle of sweat on my left temple.

I walk calmly out of the store, leaving the shop-keeper to his call. And as I walk from the store the reality of what I have just done hits me. My pace quickens, an agitated walk melts into a run, and suddenly a waterfall of kinetic energy cascades into my legs. I am on fire from the inside. I am running, I am actually running down Broadgate at 1.17 on a Thursday afternoon. Through the be-suited City boys and the teenage charity workers. The beer is in my hand now and I can feel the stares boring down into my skin, but I am running so fast that I don't care. I am a force of nature, no thought just action. I turn right at the Pizza Express on to Commercial Street and I am still going, past Barclays bank, on to Brick Lane. My legs are not connected to my mind anymore. I'm not thinking, for once I'm not thinking about anything at all. My face is covered in tangy salty sweat and my mouth is dry, I am spitting out little white flecks of foam. Suddenly a sharp pain hits just above my stomach. I have felt this before, long ago, when I was a child. Running with my cousins through Wanstead flats. It's a stitch; it's a fucking stitch. I stop and fall to my haunches, greedily wheezing at the air. I start to giggle gently like a babbling brook full of sun and movement and before I know it I am laughing, laughing from the bottom of my core, from somewhere deep inside me that I cannot regulate or switch off and for once I just go with it, howling in the middle of the afternoon, outside a dilapidated warehouse off Brick Lane.

And it's still here 23 minutes later, the lightness, as I am sitting on a park bench by Spitalfields City Farm watching the donkey and the goats chewing the grass, oblivious to everything else, living in their own world. And on first check, the world is still turning, teenagers are smoking underneath the birch trees, dappled white geese are fighting each other for the old woman's stale crumbs, City boys and secretaries stream through the park, checking their watches for the last minutes of their lunch hours. Everything is the same, but something is different, I should be going with them, but I don't. Instead I am cradling a lukewarm can of

Heineken, and I can feel the corners of my mouth folded upwards. I am smiling. My heartbeat has returned to a familiar tempo, the moisture has returned to my mouth, the first wave of the beer buzz has started to hit. And I feel light-headed, sun kissed in the autumn light. Then, like rain clouds coming in from the sea, my thoughts darken. No doubt they will smell it on my breath when I go back to the office, they will see my sweat-soaked shirt and trousers, and they might even pause to think about it for a while. But that will be it, a confusing conundrum for an afternoon soon to be replaced by some other drama in the day. Just as the old ways start to manifest, the black tentacles start to choke the beauty I have seen.

But I am saved. I am saved again by the furious sound of hope. I hear a din of teenage voices behind me. I turn away from the farm and look at the park. Thirty metres behind me a gang of boys no more than fifteen years old are playing football. Girls sit on benches talking, laughing, smoking cigarettes. The boys have cast down their blazers and their shirts hang loose, mud stains the shins of their black school trousers. They are shouting and swearing, and cursing and falling and in the receding autumn sunlight I watch them for no more than minutes. But it is enough; I have never seen anything so beautiful in my life, like staring at the face of hope. I am overcome with a sense of what the future might bring. I told you that this day was going to be different.

Wondering if you might grow a beard, nearly
overwhelmed by indifference, your cousin's ELP
albums and the promise of an early bed, you got
dead-legged by two punk girls at a Gary Glitter
concert. Then flat on your back with a can of Colt 45
listening to Siouxsie Sioux or Billy Bragg then
skanking or something at an International Marxist
Group disco trying to bite the hand that fed you
with a leaking spliff in your mouth, feeling sick and
reduced to playing John Cooper Clarke's
'Chickentown' on transparent vinyl to a class of
fourteen year olds. But at last falling backwards
from a balcony at the Hammersmith Odeon, singing
along to The Smiths. Does the mind rule the body or
does the body rule the mind?

Oliver's Army

Martin Lloyd Edwards

It was in The Headgate. Saturday night. I'd just put money in the jukebox. Greg was there, standing by the jukebox, looking like a corruptible saint, wearing a thin silvery jacket, his black hair oiled back from his high, pale forehead. He was watching a pretty boy at a nearby table. A quiet boy, drinking too much, starting to make too much noise. The boy was mouthing off about soldiers in Ireland, leaning forward, waving his hands around, chopping the air with them. 'They're just murdering bastards, an occupying force. No different from the, from the Nazis in France.'

Nobody was disagreeing with him.

'And somebody put some real music on pleeease. What is this rock'n'roll teddy boy crap?'

He shouted the word crap and some of his friends laughed.

'Shut the fuck up, Ollie,' one of them said. 'Just shut the fuck up.'

It was my song playing: Elvis. 'Heartbreak Hotel'. Ollie lurched up from his seat and across to the jukebox, which he started feeding with money: coin after coin after coin. And then punching in the code. He seemed to know it off by heart. The same code: punch, punch, punch, punch, punch, punch, again and again.

I reckoned he was probably a student from the art college: cherry red Kicker boots, hacked about hair with a dusting of green dye, earring, army surplus jacket with a plastic flower in the buttonhole. The Headgate attracted plenty like him, along with some bikers, real punks, a few older people. The jukebox was part of the attraction. For some reason it carried unusual tunes, things you wouldn't hear elsewhere: 'Gates of Eden' . . . 'Strange Fruit' . . . 'Tutti-Frutti' . . . lots of blues, reggae, punk. 'White Riot' . . . 'Hanging Garden' . . . I liked to play Elvis and 'Jean Genie' and 'Hard Rain', the Roxy Music version.

It wasn't just the jukebox that brought me to The Headgate. I liked the place because I could be pretty sure there'd be no one around who'd recognise me. And also because, of course, I knew Greg would be there. He generally liked to stand to the right of the jukebox. Small glass of Smirnoff vodka in his hand. The yellowy light from the jukebox would shine up against the side of his face, smoothing it, making him look as if he'd been shaped out of wax, some kind of gorgeous, tacky religious icon. I'd managed to pluck up the courage to stand next to him a couple of times but he'd barely glanced at me, never acknowledged that he'd sat in the passenger seat of my car, my Austin Princess, with his trousers round his ankles. As if that had never happened.

The real music Ollie had been wanting to hear was 'Oliver's Army'. There was a small cheer from his table as it started, the 'Dancing Queen' piano riff darkening into an awkward, chippy vocal:

Don't start that talking, I could talk all night.

Ollie pin-balled back from the jukebox to his table through the loosely packed bar crowd, apologising and smiling as he went, a nice smile, even teeth, and sat down again. He closed his eyes and started singing along, his friends joining in for the chorus:

Oliver's Army are on their way,
Oliver's Army are here to stay . . .

His friends looked a lot like him: a couple of boys with dyed blond hair, one wearing eyeliner, two girls about the age of my daughter and one slightly older boy in a black and red hooped Dennis the Menace sweater. They would all, I thought, almost certainly belong to bands. The older boy seemed a little embarrassed by Ollie, looking around every now and then as if hoping to see someone cooler, more interesting.

'Oliver's Army' finished. There was a pause and then it started again for the second time. Ollie's table cheered once more and Ollie stood up for a moment, swaying wildly, singing again, until someone pulled him down.

I was watching two young men over by the door. They were making me nervous. Their haircuts were army but it wasn't a place squaddies usually came. In fact I'd never seen any in there before. It really wasn't their sort of pub. They were looking across at Ollie and his group with bitter stares. One of them leaned forward from the waist and let a gob of spit fall between his feet. He looked down at it for a moment, said something from the corner of his mouth to his friend, and then rubbed the spit in to the carpet with the toe of his shoe.

For a third time 'Oliver's Army' started playing. The cheers from Ollie's table were muted. I wondered how many times he'd actually programmed the jukebox to play it. Wasn't there a limit? I liked 'Oliver's

Army' up to a point but I didn't want to listen to it all night. People were getting irritated. I watched the landlord peer over the heads of drinkers at the bar, perhaps thinking his jukebox had jammed somehow.

Greg was still gazing at Ollie, who'd stopped singing and was ranting again:

'If I was Irish I'd join the IRA. You'd have to. It would be a duty.'

He was standing up now, holding his beer glass out in front of him. Greg seemed mesmerised. I tried to catch his eye.

'Oliver's Army' finished, and then started again for the fourth time. Someone jeered and there were a few slow handclaps, petering out as the chorus kicked in again.

Oliver's Army are on their way,
Oliver's Army are here to stay . . .

There was another group, mainly young men, at a table across the other side of the room who started to sing the chorus, one of them standing up on his chair and conducting.

Ollie was still talking. And talking. I wanted to put a hand over his mouth and push him firmly, calmly, down in to his chair, out of the way. But he was getting louder, more intrusive and irritating and there was a moment as 'Oliver's Army' finished for the fourth time when his voice was suddenly amplified in the pause before the song started up yet again.

'If I had a gun now I'd go down to the barracks and do some shooting. I would. I really, really would.'

And then Elvis Costello was off again for the fifth time. The jaunty piano, the jaundiced voice. One of the bikers leaning up against the bar turned round and whistled loudly and yelled to no one in particular:

'Put something fucking else on will you?'

Ollie was oblivious to this. Not that there was much he could do. He couldn't have cancelled the songs even if he'd wanted to. His friend in the red and black hooped sweater covered his face with his hands.

The two squaddies had heard Ollie talking about doing some shooting and they weren't happy about it. It was hard to blame them. I watched them both drain glasses of lager, shaved scalps creasing thickly at the nape as heads tilted and throats worked. Would they leave or start trouble? I thought they'd probably leave.

I drained my own glass of bitter and began to move cautiously across to where Greg was standing. I wanted to be out of the way if any trouble did start. I eased myself in next to him and leant back against the wall. I was only inches away from him. I tried to make eye contact but he looked away, turning his silvery shoulder slightly, gazing across again at Ollie.

'Oliver's Army' faded and there were ironic cheers from the bikers at the bar. The pause between songs seemed longer than normal. Ollie yelled out: 'One more time?'

No one laughed. I looked to see whether the squaddies had left. There was no sign of them. And then 'Oliver's Army' did indeed start for the sixth time. Ollie was cheering and people were muttering and the landlord was coming and Greg in his silver jacket was smiling and then a loud crunch and a crash and silence.

Talking stopped. Sound of muted voices from the pub's front room, cars going past outside towards Sloman Road. And everyone looking round. The yellowy light was still smoothing Greg's wonderful cheekbones. His shaped eyebrows were lifted in theatrical horror. The mouth I'd kissed, lips I'd bitten, shaped into a frozen pink O.

The two squaddies hadn't left. They were standing with their backs to the wrecked jukebox. They'd stamped the heels of their shoes into the two brittle plastic panels on the front of the machine and looked slightly nervous now. Probably they'd only meant to make the record skip. I lowered my eyes and moved my face into shadow behind Greg. The squaddies were moving towards Ollie's table, past the landlord who was being held back by the bikers. Ollie didn't seem to realise what was about to happen. He was looking at the squaddies woozily but interestedly, as if they were approaching to engage in some heated, but essentially fair, political debate. The older boy in red and black hoops was more alert. I watched him ease his chair back from the table and slip a hand round the neck of an empty Newcastle Brown Ale bottle. The landlord had got free of the bikers and was shouting at everyone to calm down and pack it in and somebody needed to pay for his fucking jukebox.

The boy in the black and red stripes was first to make a move. He stood up and brought the bottle down against the edge of the table. He did this calmly and neatly. He knew what he was doing. He got hold of Ollie's collar and yanked him back. The squaddies stopped. Somebody was holding out a bottle for them but they ignored it. They hadn't imagined bottles.

'You wankers!' one of them spat. 'You complete wankers. You get your poncey fucking education and you don't even know its Oliver's Army is on its way. Not are, its. Its way! Its way! Its way! How many fucking armies do you think there are? My dad would be fucking ashamed if I got that wrong. Fucking ashamed.'

And then he looked to his left and saw me. Saw me half-hidden behind Greg and recognised me and saluted. He stood up straight and saluted! I stepped forward and saluted him back. What else was there to do?

'Well done soldier,' I said, 'well done,' and turning to the landlord: 'I'll see the jukebox is repaired.'

People drifted away after that. Ollie and his friends were the first to go after clearing up the broken glass from the Brown Ale bottle and Greg followed. I drank a beer with the landlord and the bikers, talking about the time I'd spent with the regiment in Ireland and Germany. And then I drove around in my Princess for a while with the radio on very quietly, looking for Greg.

Ollie and Greg were sitting together on a bench by the river. I drove past a couple of times and then parked along the street, switched off my lights and watched them. They seemed to be debating something, or at least Ollie was, moving his hands around, chopping the air. Greg wasn't saying much, just listening. He looked across at my car once or twice and at his watch. Eventually Ollie stood up and shook Greg's hand intensely with both of his and walked off, quickly, back along the river towards town. Greg gazed at my car for a long while, yawned and then stood up himself and began walking towards me. He opened the door and climbed in without saying anything, barely looking at me. He leaned forward and turned up the volume on the radio high enough so talking was out of the question. ABBA's 'Dancing Queen' was playing: *the night is young and the music's high* . . .

I started the engine, switched on the headlights and began to drive away from the town.

When I was sixteen or seventeen I saw David Hockney's Talking Heads cover hanging up in a museum. I loved David Hockney's Polaroid art, but the fact it was a record cover made me want the record, and got me into Talking Heads. I used to have a car back then and that's where I listened to music. Alone, driving fast down A1A on the Florida coast, over the bridge and into the city. The city was boring but loud music made it alright. I played this song a lot 'cos it sounded cool, you know, kind of dangerous. I liked the words and I liked the adventures I imagined. 'Cos fuck man, there was nothing going on where I was living back then.

Psycho Killer

Alison Mosshart

I was born on the same day as Billy the Kid. That's the truth. And I've always wondered if it's got anything to do with anything.

My odds felt good. I wanted to go to a casino and give away the rest. Get rid of it. My arms were fulla helium. My kidneys tickled. My fingernails itched. I was bored or I was this or I was that. My mind was full of shit. But mostly, he was pissing me off. Grinning at me, refusing to get off the bed, looking at the TV and looking at me, back and forth like that. Oh . . .

We was in El Paso like two goldfish in a bowl . . .

'I'm *too* bored now', I says. 'But even if you want me to take it out on you I won't. I just can't sit in this hotel with you, *like this*, any longer.' I couldn't look at him. 'So what channel you want me to leave the TV on? Cos I'm going out, right, and this is me trying to be nice.'

I was talking to my boy.

Before I tell you this story, there are a few things you should know. I'm not gonna tell you who we are. We ain't scared of anything, and what we're up to ain't really anybody's business. We're kinda . . . on the go.

We're looking around, see, at everything. But now and then we catch a stoplight. What happens next is often determined by nothing more than a flip of a coin, cognitively speaking.

Now I used to be a little too hopeful about what I was gonna find, and how life was gonna go. Not that I ain't hopeful now. I'm just realistic. The way I look at it, there are two sides to a coin, but there's also the middle and the crust and the dirt that gets stuck in the dips. One day you're on a mountain and you're high. The next day you're in a ditch and you're low. Then POW! Next day you're in a tunnel and the lights are out, and you're awful numb.

He and I have our differences. We argue. Yes. We curse and we fight. We never apologise. But we used to. We used to. But we musta ran out of sympathies. Maybe you get them in a limited amount when you're born. Ever wonder that? I do. Or maybe we intend every dark side we show, now that we're older and a little less hopeful.

See, me and my boy have an arrangement. We're stuck together. On account of the amount of times we've tried to get rid of each other and failed, we both know, we're tied up, and that's life. Some may see us as dark or distasteful, coiled like a snake, backward, fucked up, scum, etc. But we're just us, a tiny part of a bigger mess. The days come one at a time.

The story I'm about to tell you happened on a weekday. In the evening. The weather was hot and we both had long hair.

Well, I left my boy in the hotel room that night

and I went out walking. I got the address for the casino from the phonebook, under the Bible in the drawer by the bed, like how it always is. There was an ad for it but I knew it was gonna be a dud really, you know, like a small-time crime casino in the back of a restaurant/bar/apartment. Cash only sweet Jesus and enough dirt in the carpet to trip on.

I called them up and it went through to an old lady's house somewhere else. She was acquainted with the error and was annoyed but too old and tired to hang up the phone right, and she dropped it. BANG. Take a hint.

Look, I didn't even have enough money to truly get involved, or the skills. The casino thing isn't really my thing but I was yearning for the senselessness and the desperation of it, somebody else's maybe, not my own. That night I felt funny. I knew I was gonna lose. I knew this, and it felt good. I was in control. I was in a real good mood then, thinking about that.

When I find myself in a new town full of people I don't know, what I do when I open the door to a place I never been, I go for the thing maybe least conspicuous and I act very casual like I own the joint anyway, like it's my normal routine to be where I am, and I sit down at the bar. Just like that. I pull my collar up and I look around like it's my joint and I light a cigarette like it's my joint and I wait for the ashtray to be delivered to me. This gets the interaction going. They come to me.

So I'm at the casino. I'm sitting there and there's a cowboy about 65 with a beer in one hand and a blonde girl's ass in the other. He's sitting a few seats away. The bartender's got cut off jean shorts, horse teeth, straight thin brown hair, crucifix around her neck, the usual. Nothing about this joint is classy. I'm in a great mood and here comes my ashtray along with a bowl of potato chips she pushes down my way. She asks me what I want to drink with all the coloured lights in her eyes and I say, 'a greyhound, OK.'

Well she looks down the bar after looking at me, as if to say, 'Look at that,' and I look over too, again, and she looks back at me and shakes her head and says, 'He's an old dirty man and she's a stupid floozy.' And I think to myself, 'Who in the world uses the word floozy these days?'

Well she calls herself Roberta.

Now, as I intended, I act like I know where I'm going and walk into the backroom with my drink. It's like I thought. Dark. Just about empty. There's a card table but the dealer has his walkman on and he's watching the football game over my head. There's a couple of slot machines. I figure I don't need anyone for that and start there. Six dollars down and nothing's happening. Greyhound is gone. Things are going well in my opinion.

I head back to Roberta. The cowboy and the blonde girl are eating the potato chips and I take note that Blondy is absolutely shit-faced. So drunk, she just keeps saying, 'Hank Hank Hanky I'm hunga.' Hungry I guess. Roberta fumbles and drops the greyhound she's making me sideways into the ice bucket. She looks at it for way too long. I'm talking days she's looking. Finally she lets out a big fat 'MOTHER FUCKER!' Sure enough the kitchen door swings wide open and big boy boss heads over to have a look.

'Shit, Roberta,' he says.
'Shit, Bob!'
'Shit, Roberta!'
'Shit, Bob!'
'Roberta . . . '
'Shit.'

I kid you not, that was the conversation. They started changing out the whole ice bucket and forgot about me. I forgot about them too and watched the cowboy smoke his cigar and lean back on his stool and rub his belly like he'd just won life's fucking lotto and all was good with the world. He burped and looked pleased with that. The Blonde girl was reapplying her lipstick and hopping around on liquid legs. Suddenly the front door burst open and in walked a very hairy man. The hairiest man I have ever seen. His face looked like ten mops bundled together.

And I knew he was gonna run straight to me and sure enough he did. Came boot stomping over with a black cloud above him like the meanest hurricane you ever seen and all the palm trees are back bending so low you can pick the coconuts off 'em while you're sitting on the floor. In real slow motion his mouth unzipped and he let out a wail . . .

'Your boy!' he says, 'is down at the dairy with a pistol and he's shooting the joint up! He's really going to town! He says to get you. Your name's Sue, right?'

Well I was shaking my head YES and NO at the same time, partially cos I had no goddamn clue what my boy was calling me that given day. But I knew he was meaning me.

'He's at the dairy on fourth, you better get there quick and try and . . . .'

The lights in my head went dark . . .

And the rest that Hairy was saying just got real blurry to me. I just seen him sweating and panting and bright red under his hairy mask and blabbering to me like we'd been neighbours for years and my house was on fire and it was about to catch his house on fire, meanwhile he's throwing all his clothes and furniture out onto his front lawn and calling me a bitch at the same time . . . Suddenly I focused and I noticed a bit of scrambled egg caught on his face . . . hair . . . face hair, whatever.

Well now Roberta's eyes were burnin' a hole through my temple and the cowboy had spun right round on his stool and was looking too and the blonde girl had fallen to the floor with a dizzy grin on her face and her hair was swimming around in the cowboys spilt beer and the card dealer walked into the bar and pulled his walkman off an' looked at me like I'd robbed him in his sleep. My instinct was to get the pistol from my purse and stop all their staring but something said to me don't so I didn't, and I got up and flew.

Now I didn't even know this town but I was running down the street looking for numbers and I ran the wrong way and out came Hairy yelling even more and pointing wildly in the other direction. Once on course, I got to the dairy on fourth pretty quick, and sure enough the windows were out. There were holes everywhere. Food on the floor and the cook too, looking pretty cooked. Dead as it gets. And the coffee was dripping from the plaster panelling in the ceiling mixing with the blood, and some eggs were still frying and burning real bad and stinking yellow black and red and my boy wasn't there but the cops were rolling up. By that I mean one sheriff in a Ford Taurus hit the curb going too fast and knocked right into the corner of the dairy, made me jump. Though I'd done nothing, I started running back to the hotel. I ran like the wind.

Now that black cloud was hanging over *my* head, and I was mad.

(Stop.)

You see we're not exactly travelling. If you want to know the truth, which I ain't really gonna tell you, it's something like this: we're looking for somewhere that can stand us. And by that I mean, somewhere we're gonna blend in, somewhere that don't put either of us too much on edge. We're looking for a place with no sharp corners, no dark shadows, and no need for us whatsoever.

Now this was the 43rd city in nine years and all this was going through my mind as I was running. Cos I was hopeful enough to think maybe we'd made it. But like I said, the older I get, the less hopeful I am. I don't fall as hard as I used to. I void various levels of hope just about as easy as some people cross out dates on a calendar counting down to a birthday or a court date, or what have you. I cross cities off the map and watch the world shrink.

(OK, continue . . .)

I was kind of hesitant opening up the door to the hotel room you know then, cos my boy must've been angry to have done what he did. He sure was having some kind of maddening joyride at the expense of our ease in that town. And all I could think of was something on the TV made him itch, or I did, by leaving. The latter,

I thought, was the greater possibility. So I opened the door to the room slowly. And I could see his legs on the bed. And I opened it more and I could see his torso. And I opened it all the way and I could see his head, and he was asleep.

Well I woke him up with a big rattling shake of the bed and I asked what was going on with him and the dairy and why'd he felt so much a need to do what he did. He opened his eyes and smiled and said I got some kind of sense of humour. Now he and I both know, I don't have too much of a sense of humour these days, at least not concerning him.

I told him the cook was dead and he flipped the channel on the TV like a psycho and stopped it on a re-run soap opera. I was clenching my jaw so much I could feel my teeth turning to dust. He had the nerve to say to me under his breath, over the soap, that I was *damn* sick. And in soap-land, Kelly was angry at Susan for not visiting Michelle in the hospital but little did she know, Michelle had been sleeping with Kelly's husband and Susan knew this, so out of respect to Kelly, didn't visit. But we'd seen this one before.

Well of course he denied everything about that night. But I can look at my boy's face anytime on any given day and read right into what he's been up to, in detail, in the last 48 hours or however much I need to know. If only to annoy him, I carried on with my questions . . . I mentioned the hairy man and his body convulsed with laughter. I knew for certain, he sent the hairy man to find me as a joke.

So we packed our bags and loaded them into the car and it was raining like hell and I was sitting in the driver's seat and he was messing around in the trunk and I put the car in reverse and I was gonna back right over him full speed, flatten him right out, cos I felt the need to. This is one of my more common urges, you know, a thought that crosses my mind at least once a week. Killing him would be easy to do.

The police were passing us by now, and an ambulance too, maybe a fire truck, and this caught my attention and I forgot to kill him. He got in the car and I looked at him and I felt like giving him a kiss, and he probably felt like that too but I lost that feeling when I looked in the mirror and saw a sheriff looking through the back window. So I rolled out of that parking lot going about 65 backwards straight onto the highway and the thump I heard coulda' been a man or a log or something, but I don't know. Whatever it was never caught up with us.

I remember my boy asked me if I'd won anything at the casino and I said NO and he thought that was a shame and we argued about this until we caught the next stoplight.

The days come one at a time.

That was just a Thursday in El Paso.

"

I first heard this song one summer in the 1980s. At the time I was a teen singer in a post-punk band and lived in a disused chocolate factory on the banks of the Rhine. Our rehearsal space was a windowless bunker that the guitarist said was left over from the war – the concrete walls made good soundproofing. I had no idea, back then, what inspired The Dead Kennedys to write the song. To my ears it was just a rollicking hardcore anthem and the discord in the notes was a match for the times.

"

California Über Alles

Lane Ashfeldt

You must be hungry when you pick up the bar of chocolate off the floor and slip your finger under the dusty red wrapper with its gold crown logo. You are wishing, maybe, that your stuff hadn't got nicked and that you were in a real factory in Berlin earning the mythical eight Deutschmarks an hour Jarleth said he'd get for his summer job, instead of here in a dead factory in Köln, earning nothing.

The chocolate bar in your hand seems odd. Old-fashioned. The oblong packet is decorated with swirls and scrolls, gold lettering that spells out flavours and ingredients you don't understand the names of. The chocolate you have bought in local shops looks nothing like this; square in shape, it comes in seven or eight flavours, *Vollmilch*, *Vollnuß*, *Sport*, *Pfefferminz* and so on, each in its own resealable wrapper. The one you like best has Rice Krispies inside. The resealable wrappers – intended to signify that you needn't be fat to eat chocolate – never in fact reseal very convincingly, but this doesn't bother you since you'd rather eat a whole bar in one go. At this moment, however, you definitely don't feel fat. You haven't eaten since yesterday lunch. The hard tug in your gut that you felt on waking has gone now, replaced by a certain dreamy light-headedness.

Before you even glance at what's under this wrapper you know it won't taste as good as one of those Rice Krispie bars, but on the other hand it's here, it's free, and you're hungry. You discard the tacky wrapper and lift the gold paper. It is then that you see: beneath it, the chocolate is a dusty greyish white.

You have no English word to adequately express your disappointment, so you try a new word, a word you say long and low as you've heard your German punk friends say it: *Scheiße*. The hard 'i' works well for swearing, you are thinking; why 'shite' sounds stronger than 'shit'. But with its hiss of sibilant leading to a tiny second syllable, *Scheiße* is strongest of all, even said whisper-soft.

Although parts of the falling-down but beautiful factory have been water damaged and this room seems especially damp, although you know you shouldn't eat anything found here, you don't hurl the chocolate bar on the floor. Instead you glare at it minutely, holding it inches from your face.

The squares protrude awkwardly from a base that is wider on one side than on the other, as if the makers got the maths slightly wrong when fixing the mould. You remember the perfect symmetry of the chocolate bars in the shops and think to yourself, did this factory go bust because it couldn't keep up with the competition? Did its owners have so much faith in their grandiose, old-style chocolate that they carried on churning it out past the point when anyone was willing to pay for it? You imagine what it must be like to go bust this spectacularly. To own these huge buildings in the centre of downtown Köln, right on the riverfront in the Altstadt Süd, and finally not be able to shift any product. To close down leaving behind hundreds of unsold chocolate bars going white under their wrappers in various parts of the factory, and an artillery of heavy-duty machines that once mixed chocolate, or printed paper wrappers. Machines that stand untended now, their metal feet rusting in puddles that have formed where the roof or pipes have begun to disintegrate.

You break off a square of chocolate and examine it. Beneath the layer of white, the chocolate is still dark brown. And, you notice optimistically, it still smells sweet.

Downstairs, in another part of the *Schokoladenfabrik*, a band plays softly. It's only the support act, no one worth seeing. Some acoustic guitar duo or trio, friends of the hippies. But, later, Dietz's band is playing. Them you do mean to see. You saw them bring in their gear for the sound check earlier and noticed that the blond boy was with them, the boy whose name you don't know yet, the boy with the laughing eyes. Later, you tell yourself, you will go down and see what's going on: *was ist los*, *wie geht's*, *was gibt's*? But first you have to stop feeling so damn hungry you can't even stand up. You definitely won't understand what people are saying to you, much less be able to say anything in response, unless you eat something. Again you look at the dusty grey bar and wonder if you can do this.

Gingerly, you bite into it, ready to spit if it tastes bad. The square gives way and releases a nasty marzipan goo, but the actual chocolate tastes fine, if a little . . . dry. You examine the place where your bite mark is and see that the bar had a three-stage construction: milk chocolate base, then the goo, dark chocolate on top. The base is the bit you like best. Next time you bite along the edges to avoid the gooey squares. Sweetness explodes in your mouth, swells until your tongue sticks to your palate. You have nothing to drink and there is no running water on this level, so you slip your tongue around your teeth to make your mouth water, so you can swallow some more.

You look at the hundreds of bars of perfectly edible chocolate, and do a little mental dance. It seems like a lifetime supply.

You don't yet know that, come midsummer (a rainy Kölnische midsummer not much warmer than the Irish ones you're used to), you will tear open the remaining bars of chocolate and find only oblongs of polystyrene, display items made to withstand melting in the shop windows of some warmer city.

You don't yet know that the boy with the badly dyed blond hair will start going with another girl, and that after this you will leave the chocolate factory for a job on the Kölner-Düsseldorfer Linie, bringing American tourists to see castles along the banks of the Rhine. From the porthole of the cramped cabin you share with another teenage girl, Üte, you will witness the concrete globes and funnels of the nuclear power stations that are also parked along the river's edge; against your wishes you will stare at them, held by their mesmeric simplicity. More majestic, more awe-inspiring than the castles, as if they have always been there and always will be. Machine smooth, untouchable by *Atomkraft nein danke* protests, untouchable by humans, untouchable by time. You will feel a chill as the boat passes in their shadow.

When, after a week of travelling up and down the river, the boat again berths in Köln for the night, you will rush off to the chocolate factory where you will find the blond boy fighting with another punk. A real physical fight, and when afterwards he catches your eye, all the laughter will be gone from his. Everyone will be bored and broke that night, and you won't have been paid yet. (The tips left by American tourists are no use, since they give them in the small change of countries they have already passed through, countries you may never even visit.) So, from the main hall where the old alkos lie sleeping, you and *die kleine* Marion will gather all the empty beer bottles you can find and carry them around the corner to the bar. There, the barman will allow you 20 pfennigs against each of sixteen empties. He will set three full bottles of beer on the wooden counter between you, and beside them a single yellow 20 pfennigs piece that will land with a spin. Before the coin has finished its dance he will turn away, thinking the transaction complete.

Gib mal mehr, Marion will shout, pulling out a gun and pointing it at the barman.

You will have seen this gun before. The blond boy passed it round the circle once while a group of you sat smoking joints and listening to Joy Division and Stiff Little Fingers, which you knew was his favourite band since the letters SLF were painted large on his black leather jacket. Your hand lowered as the cold metal sank heavily into your palm, and you knew then that the gun was real, but in that context it also seemed strangely unreal. A phantom from the past, perhaps from the war, a time-traveller gun. You turned it over and read the word Luger, saw initials scratched by hand on the barrel. Then you passed it on. When the song ended the gun was forgotten, relegated to the uncertain time zone where it once held sway.

But this time is different. This time the whole bar will change unforgettably in a second, in a very here-and-now kind of way: a barstool lifted high, your friend hit over the head with it. You try to shout that it's just her idea of a joke, that the gun's not loaded, but you don't know the German for loaded and everything happens so fast it is like watching speeded up film.

Someone will raise a stool to hit you too, but you will back into a corner and in moments the police will arrive to arrest *die kleine* Marion. She will say nothing to you as they take her away. It will be as if she doesn't even see you. You will feel bad and tell one of the police you were with her, but he will ask if it was you who pulled the gun, and when you say no he will laugh harshly and tell you to go home and behave.

In less than a summer, less than six weeks even, all this will be simple past to you. For now, it's unimaginable, almost, and yet when it comes – while it's actually happening in the present tense – none of it really surprises you, not even the thing with the gun. It's no more crazy than people without homes taking over one of the city's dead spaces and using it. It's just that that was crazy in a good way, and the thing with the gun is crazy in a bad way.

You spend a lot of time thinking, that summer. Half-formed thoughts, not really in English or in German, thoughts that don't really belong either in this country or the one you've left behind. Dazed impressions. About *Deutsch Amerikanische Freundschaft*, what it means now (an obscure but fashionable band) and what it meant before (something about the postwar relationship, about the Germans having to pay off their war debt). You are surprised to see American soldiers in Germany, surprised again to note that they are all black, because in the war movies you have seen on TV the soldiers are never black. You think of how losers over time become winners, of how wealthy Japan and

Germany have become, and you wonder how long the decline of the American empire will take. That summer, you expect to watch it unfold in the space of the next few years – but back then you think you will live forever. Forever. And still be dead before the year 2000.

The electricity doesn't work in this part of the building. Across on the other side of the river the last streaks of daylight glow yellow and turquoise above the city rooftops. A single dark ribbon of cloud furls itself above the horizon in what is otherwise a completely clear sky, and a phrase from your German textbook echoes through your head, an example of the future tense: *es wird bald dunkel*. (It becomes soon dark.)

You turn from the window and make for the stairs, stopping only to take one more bar of chocolate and stuff it in your pocket. You are halfway downstairs when the vague tuning-up noises you have been hearing give way to something louder and more definite. The last two flights you take at a run. When you get there Dietz is pogoing on the small stage in unselfconscious mimicry of bands he loves from other parts of the world. You hear an eruption of metal, energy and feedback, a rush of audio fallout that causes several hippies to retreat somewhere quieter where they can continue their endless *diskutieren*. But to you these twisted sounds are full of hope; their harsh cynicism and skewed logic make sense to you right now.

And at this moment, listening to Dietz cover a Dead Kennedys song, you are firmly rooted in the present. You are looking at the boy with the badly dyed blond hair, the boy whose name you still don't know. He is playing bass guitar. You hold up a bar of chocolate to him, '*Willst du?*' and he nods '*Klar*', looking back at you with his laughing eyes, so you reach over and place the unopened bar of chocolate on the guitar amp next to him.

The song goes on: a song based on the old German national anthem, the one they're not allowed to sing any more. A song that started as a joke but will end by being truer than you suppose. *California über alles, über alles, California, Da-da-da-da-da-DA-da, Da-da-da-da-da-DA-da*.

Patrik Fitzgerald was a bit of a punk oddity, a lone singer with an acoustic guitar was a rare occurrence in 1977. Often described as the Bob Dylan of punk, he wrote songs and poems that spoke of alienation, sorrow and realism. He was a true punk poet, whose early songs like 'Safety Pin Stuck in My Heart' sound as relevant now as they ever did.

Safety Pin Stuck in My Heart

Janine Bullman

The first time I saw them, they were sitting a few seats in front of me on the top deck of a 55 bus. They'd got on at Old Street across from Hoxton Town Hall. Him all skinny limbs, legs bathed in denim, his feet on the seat, head resting on his knees, a wonky haircut and a slinky arm wrapped around a girl. Her with a shock of dyed black poker-straight hair reaching down to nowhere, blunt fringe, seamed tights like a black marker up the back of her thighs, disappearing under a short black skirt. Her head resting on his shoulder, they sat in silence, didn't say a word to each other. They didn't need to. There was something about them reminded me of us . . . the fever and the silence that can lie between two people.

Two weeks later I saw them again on Mare Street by the railway bridge. I was on the bus again, this time heading into Shoreditch, it was a Saturday night around seven. I was planning on having a drink and then another. I could see spilt milk spewing across the pavement by her feet. She was in tears, calling out to him; he was further down the road, those scrawny legs walking away from her. Then I remembered this is how love begins, broken hearted in Hackney or Liverpool or Leeds or wherever. Later on behind closed doors it will be made up in hot kisses like water to quench the anguish.

Ever since July my days and nights felt raw, like red meat, like neat vodka, sharpening my vision of hell. And as I drifted further into that night I kept thinking about the couple. Him with the crippled hair cut. Her red wine lips and locks like a velvet midnight mile, and I'd have another drink and think about their love, how it must be for them, and I'd try to forget about the one I'd lost.

I'd keep drinking till it blistered inside of me putting a wash across my eyes, so by the time I was heading home, I could no longer see straight. Blind folded in the wrap of night it was like someone had switched out the lights. The hours had dropped away like shadows, I could feel the pavement slipping from under my feet and like a fainting trapeze artist everything turns black and I go into freefall. All I could hear was the sound of laughter rattling in alleyways, cars sizzling across wet tarmac; I could sense the damp air from the rain and see the blur of street lamps rippling through pools on the pavement as I flipped, uncoiled reeling like a banshee into the wasteland, coughing and spluttering into the dawn of the next day. I was clutching at lampposts and holding onto anyone who would hold onto me; after all isn't this the British way, a Saturday night spent looking for meaning in the bottom of a glass, in whatever is going to leave me disillusioned on Kingsland Road at 2am?

When I make it home I will be falling through the door and through the floor and just falling. Each time the same, clutching on to the toilet bowl puking up the grief and the guilt, the suppressed and the repressed choking in my gullet. Most of the next day spent with eyes down searching through the cracks in the floorboards looking for some light. Racking my brains wondering how we got so lost, how our love became debased? Do you judge the love by the lover, if so what grade was I? What standard did I reach?

Every breath rattling inside of me, was it possible to ache more than this? Our hearts are delicate organs and Jesus he had twisted mine into some unfathomable shape and then when he had dragged me through it all, his own heart had stopped like a clock in the night.

From what I know it was a night like any other, no different to this night or last or the countless ones before. I was told he fell asleep, watching an episode of *The Two Ronnies*. Sleeping in an old iron bed that we'd found together in a junk shop in Rye back in a time when things were different. And here in the middle of that ordinary night, peacefully sleeping, it ended without a fight or a scream or a sigh, 35 years and it ends. Without warning his breath slipped out for the last time and we are now history. The doctors, they never could explain what makes a healthy young man's heart stop in the middle of an average English summer night. And neither could they explain what it is like to be a woman left behind.

I wasn't there for him at the end; to suddenly wake in the night and know something was wrong, to see that his body was no longer rising and falling, to place my head on his chest and realise his heart was no longer softly ticking. I wasn't there because he had already left me behind, eight months earlier he had gone. I didn't need a doctor to tell me why he had died, because I knew. His heart broke because he left the woman he loved for another he hardly knew, then realised he couldn't turn back, that there was no way back from Southend to me, to home, not now. That beating clock of his shattered and now all our past is like rotting celluloid film. And me, well I am tired of dreaming of him, because my own heart won't stop banging.

See the problem was neither of us were willing to let the other go, however hard one would kick and scream, the other would just hold on twice as hard, knuckles turning white with the strain. It was like a game, I never saw it ending. The day you moved out you called to say you had made a mistake and then every day for eight months you called to say, 'It's not too late to try again, you know.' But for me our romance was like newspapers left out in the rain, life felt like it was unravelling stitch by stitch, one for every day of the ten years we had been together.

In those months after he left I would come home from work each night and light a fire in the grate and sit and watch the flames as they roared and hissed, lapping and licking at the charred logs, the coal embers glowing, fizzing and spitting. The room heavy with the smell of smoke, the heat cloying at the cold. It is here that I would switch the memories on, close my eyes and watch the images roll, like some form of twisted pornography for the mind, like my own TV show. I would sit staring into the fire remembering the night I came home dressed in a red Macintosh blemished black by the rain, it was in the days just before he left, the days I couldn't get warm when I just shivered. That night when I walked in the door, he took me in his arms and told me he could smell the rain on my hair and how it reminded him of summer holidays in England together. Still then we would meet in Piccadilly every Thursday evening, and every time we held each other's hands even though we were no longer together, because it is what we had always done. We held hands through it all, it's what we did best. But some things we just never did well, like knowing when enough was enough and for him telling the truth, because he knew how much it hurt.

And so he died that dank and dreary summer; like steel submarines the rain clouds lumbered over London, I would walk the broken paving stones of this city and wash my shattered thoughts out in the rain. Summer merged into autumn, soon it was November. The streets were a sludge of fallen leaves and stagnant rain, the rows of red brick houses looked dull in the grey winter light, the trees empty. The air so cold it would scratch at my lungs and settle in my hair like a ghost. I felt like I was just waiting.

See there is only me that holds those memories like some great big computer registering all the fuck-ups and the people you fucked and the ones you fucked over and the ones who fucked over you. Can anyone possibly say they don't regret, that mended hearts don't sometimes ache, that it is best to see the scars when in doubt of the wounded? Sometimes I think it's frivolous to only protest about love, I wonder if I am wasting precious breath, but I can't really see what else matters in this life; if we don't hold onto that then what else do we hold onto?

And so dusk comes each day, like a hand with broken fingers across eyelids, the sun drops away and the hours they come caressing, lapping like fear on the inky shore of night. I stare into the matt black, with the mind of an acrobat, listening to the whine of fox cubs and the breeze tangled in the trees, as the stillness of the night ebbs into the ethereal eggshell blue of dawn. In these long corridors of night, my mind walks with you in our hometown, the place where we met, where once the ships came in, where now I only seem to drown. Lime Street, Hardman Street, Catherine Street to home. I am holding onto your cold filthy hand so tightly, your fingernails engrained with dirt. And here like a storm of wild bees all the harsh words and all the heartache is rushing through my mind and all the time we never had and the time we wasted. It is here in the drawing of our days I lie waiting for the sound of footsteps, your key in the door, but this house feels like a swamp and I am trying to forget, because there comes a time when you must walk away, whilst you still can.

So now each morning on my way to work and each evening on my return, I sit on the bus watching the world just trickle past; the office blocks newly built and empty, the fried chicken shops, the off-licences, the corner shops, the neon-lit pole dancer on the side of the Metropole bar, flashing on/off/on, the Salvation Army and London Fields Station and the undertakers and the garage and the Children's Museum and the teenagers on mountain bikes and the ones with the prams and this is all reassurance that the world goes on and it walks past us daily on every street, never really looking us in the eye. And if I ever see that couple again, how I want to shake them and tell them to hold onto each other so fucking tightly and not to let go however hard it gets, because what have the young ever cared about other than shagging and drifting and forgetting? Because I didn't see the end coming. Some nights when I look through the window of the bus, down onto the passing streets below, I see a woman with a broken mouth and redundant eyes looking back at me and then I realise.

I first heard Patti Smith played on Mark Radcliffe's graveyard Radio 1 shift when I was fourteen and immediately started saving up to buy *Horses*. For me, 'Redondo Beach' is exactly what every punk song should be: completely unpredictable. After all, what could have been less likely to come out of the 70s New York rock scene than a lesbian reggae torch song?

Redondo Beach

Krissi Murison

Really, it should have been obvious what had happened, even to a fool like me. That's the thing about conclusions though: they're the last place you'll jump to when it might actually be prescient to do so.

I'd had my fair few scares with Angel before. Slapping through puddles at 4am in bare feet and crying her name until my voice cracked, only to get back home and find her there. Twisted up in the bed sheets, broken, exhausted and tiny, but soon giggling again despite herself and everything that had been said. I never learned to stop looking for her. Not until that morning on Redondo Beach. But like I said, that's the thing about conclusions: when something real and terrible is standing in front of you screaming, you'll convince yourself anything if it means you can keep looking the other way. Which is how I came to spend 45 minutes wandering up and down Catalina Avenue before the panic hit.

Panic comes in many colours; the strangling grey that can flatten you for a lifetime; the flushed crimson that swoops down to save the day, to bare its teeth or fly you straight on out of there. Right now, I was being swiftly and expertly incapacitated by the white. The hue of no redeeming features, that makes your guts plummet, kicks your feet out from under you, turns the walls inside out, and shines a pulsing light behind your eyeballs until you're blind. It was when I was still climbing the stone stairs back to the hotel room that it must have set in. But it wasn't until I stumbled through the door, past the empty, twisted bed sheets and called out her name five times – in a ten-foot by twelve-foot hotel room – that I even realised I felt it.

'How am I supposed to find her, if I can't see anything?' A chink of sense cut through the snowstorm behind my eyes. 'How am I supposed to find something as small and precious as Angel?' Then something else barged it out the way: 'Mustn't call her Angel, mustn't call her Angel . . .' Typical, my mind opens up just wide enough for a fraction of rational thought to squeeze its way through, and all I can do is fill it with the dumbest thing I can think of. I threw open the door to the bathroom in agitation and snatched back the shower curtain. Nothing. Of course, nothing. What was I expecting? Her to be lounging back in a pool of bubbles, giggling in spite of herself?

And yet maybe it wasn't so dumb. 'Don't call me Angel': she'd never liked it. Used to shrug my arm off and pull a tight face whenever I said it, like, 'Don't be the latest in a lifetime of people to just see what you want to see.' Then she'd storm out of sight, unhinging doors behind her to go stand outside in the yard and talk to the wind or whatever it was she did out there when she felt the inside world wasn't listening.

I first met her ten months ago when she was in twelfth grade and I was employed to cut the lawns at her school. I used to watch her walk home with this group of jocks and assholes and long for her to realise she didn't belong. Then one day last June she must have because she came past alone and a combination of the heat and red panic made me call out to her. I remember her looking back at me, face on one side, quizzical, like 'Hey, do I know you?' But before she had time to find the question, the fight had overtaken the flight and I was suddenly right next to her, leaning in close, my lips pushing hard against hers as she stumbled back into the mesh of the soccer pitch, trying to keep her footing. Then she gasped and leapt back and I think I probably did the same. When she ran off without saying anything I thought, 'Oh Jesus, I'm about to get myself a kicking here,' but two days later she came past that way alone again and stuck around longer. That was the night when she told me that she'd never been kissed by a girl before, and I said I'd never been the one to do the kissing before so this was new territory for everyone. Then a few weeks later there was another revelation, when she got all wobbly and teary explaining how one of the assholes she'd hung around with used to be her boyfriend, and wouldn't let it go. She'd stopped answering his phone calls, so he'd started coming to her house late at night and telling people they were going to get married after they graduated. He even bought her a ring. Angel hadn't told him why she'd called it off – about the two of us – because she was worried what effect a bombshell like that might have on a man like him, but she knew she wouldn't be able to stop him finding out soon. Nor her father who she'd found deep in filial conversation with him in their front room one night when she came home late from messing around on the pitches with me. But anyway, she said, she was tough enough to handle it if ever they did find out. And I made some joke about a little angel like her not even being tough enough to beat the fourth graders in a fight and bought her another drink.

Back in the hotel room, I grabbed at the phone and got the operator's voice. 'Please help me, I'm . . .' I managed before slamming the receiver back in its cradle and slumping to the floor. Help me what, exactly? Patch things up with my girlfriend who called me a cold arrogant bitch outside the Whole Foods Market this afternoon. The same girlfriend who then went missing because she's a highly strung fantasist with a predilection for wandering off when she doesn't think I'm taking her seriously enough? See, there I went again, refusing to admit for a second that what she told me back there might have been worth paying attention to. Oh God, no! There are few occasions in life when having a highly strung fantasist as a life partner is the best case scenario, but even the operator, if I talked the options through with her, would have to admit as much on this occasion. Not that I did. Instead I picked up Angel's denim jacket that was hanging off the edge of the bed, wrapped it around myself, and headed out the door.

Later when it was too late, I would half-remember seeing the women rushing out of the stores, crowding round in groups, pointing across to the ocean. Or the ambulance sweeping off left along the coastal road – no sirens, no lights, just a sleek, unstoppable progress that

I matched as I blazed back along South Catalina Avenue on a mission of my own.

Right now, though, I was busy half-remembering some other stuff too late. Her odd detachment over dinner, how she'd gulped at her gin and soda, turned her nose up at the menu and after a few false starts at telling me what was going on, announced that she was tired and needed to lie down, scraping her chair noisily as she left. Or how I'd come home three nights ago to find her sitting on the cold floor, the phone by her feet, sobbing and begging to go somewhere he couldn't call or skulk to watch her as she walked home. So we came twenty miles out to Redondo, checked in at the Pier Inn for the three nights my credit card would allow. What we'd do after that, I don't think either of us had figured out. Maybe that's what I thought she was busy doing when I woke up at 4am on that second night and found her missing. It wasn't unusual for her to go off wandering in the middle of the night – hell, it wasn't unusual for her to go off wandering any time of the day – and I didn't lose any sleep over it. Besides, when I came round again at 5.45, she was twisted back up in the bed sheets where she'd started the night. 'Welcome back, Angel,' I whispered, brushing her pale hair away from her closed eyes. 'Everything's going to be fine.'

By the time I'd done another sweep of South Catalina Avenue, there was no more distracting myself from the idea that things weren't going to be fine. I knew by now that what she'd been trying to tell me a few hours ago was the truth and, for the first time all day, I even knew what I had to do next. I found a payphone and called her home. I'd never introduced myself to her family, not even in the safety of a phone line. Her mother always answered and I never left my name. They had their routine and I had mine. But today I already knew it would be her father who picked up.

'Juliana?' his voice blurted out, cutting off the first ring. Juliana was her real name.

'Sorry no, is she there?' I asked, even though, as with everything else now, I already knew the answer.

'No. Who is this?' His voice was urgent. Panicked.

'A friend of hers. She was meant to be meeting me today at the beach but she hasn't turned up.'

'When you find her tell her she needs to get in touch with her mother and me immediately.'

I swallowed hard and my silence seemed to make him want to keep talking. 'There's been . . . there's been some bad news.'

'Oh God. Is there anything I can tell her?'

'There was a break-in at Brendan's house in the early hours of this morning . . .' Brendan was the ass-hole's name. 'There was a struggle and Brendan was . . .' Here his voice disappeared and I counted to five before he spoke again. 'I think it's best if you just tell her to call home the moment you see her.'

So it was true. She'd done what she said she'd done. You can't blame me for not believing her though, can you? I mean, what would you say if you were walking down the street one late afternoon and your girlfriend admitted that the reason she hadn't been in bed between the hours of 2.45 and 5am was because she'd been out bludgeoning her ex-lover to death? The guy she once planned to marry after graduation. The guy who now waited around corners to beg, plead and eventually intimidate her into taking him back. The guy who said that if he ever caught her with someone else he'd kill the both of them. And because Angel, unlike me, understood the importance of listening to people, she knew he was telling the truth. So she took a metal bar from out of his yard, broke through the back window and stopped him. So go on then, what would you say to that? Probably exactly what I said: 'You, Angel, a murderer? I don't think you've got it in you.' Then I laughed and put my arm around her, and she shrugged it off and pulled her face tight and begged, pleaded for me to listen. Because the police would come soon, she said, and we had to find somewhere else to be. Because they'd ask questions that she wouldn't be able to answer because she was such a bad liar. I could see the panic in her face, but I couldn't stop laughing – especially not at that last bit – and that's when she called me a bitch. Well at least that stopped me laughing. I shook my head, shouted that she needed to get a grip of herself and walked off. Off down Catalina Avenue to get a coffee and ignore the real and terrible conclusion screaming in front of me.

I put the phone down carefully in the receiver this time and leant back on the phonebox glass, waiting to work out what to do next. I needed to go back to the hotel. She was scared and needed me – she'd told me that when she told me everything else. Besides, it would be dark in a few hours and I'd never be able to find her out here then.

The women were still there when I walked back past the turning to the coast and I had to push right through one group of them to get past. 'Pretty little girl', one of them wailed as I tried not to listen. Seemed like I wasn't the only one to get some bad news today.

The hotel reception was empty when I walked in and I shuddered, imagining the police upstairs waiting for Angel to break the news we both now knew. I wanted to slip up the stairs unseen, but the desk clerk had other ideas. 'Excuse me,' he called out and it took me half a second to unfreeze myself enough to face him. 'Don't you need your key?'

'Sorry, I . . .' I fumbled around in my pocket for the room key I'd forgotten to leave earlier and waved it at him in explanation.

He was about my age. Spotless and proficient, but not so professional he couldn't be distracted from the job in hand.

'I take it you've heard what happened at the beach today,' he began, ignoring the key, 'with the ambulance?'

Now it was my turn to look quizzical.

'Ahhh . .' he said and stared at a spot on the desk in front of us, moving his head slowly from side to side. 'They found a girl washed up on the beach. Suicide it looked like. One of the women from the stores outside found her.'

'Oh, the woman . . .' I began, finally half-remembering. 'I heard a woman talking about it.'

'Yeah, a small, pretty blonde thing,' and here his eyes came back up to meet mine. 'I saw her with my own eyes before the ambulance took her away. Can't have been more than seventeen. She looked like an angel, really.'

A bolt of nausea caused me to fall backwards and I grabbed the front of the desk to steady myself.

'Are you OK?'

'Don't call her Angel!' I wanted to scream so loud into his face that it flailed the skin from the bone. But nothing swooped down to bare its teeth and save the day. No red, no white, not even any grey. This is what it feels like when there's nowhere left to jump, I thought, and put the key back in the pocket of her jacket and headed for the ocean.

I first fell in love with Buzzcocks via Parbold village library. The cassette of *Singles Going Steady* gleamed at me from among all the Mills and Boons and the local true crime mysteries. I loved the mad scramble of their music and the flat northernness of their vocals. I was maybe eleven or twelve then, of an age to be discovering the world beyond my home, my school, the streets where I had grown up, and so I was stirred by the petulance of punk. For me, 'Time's Up' sums up all the impatience of both punk and adolescence in general; it's raw and rough and eager to get going, nervous to be doing something, anxious to move before its time is up.

Time's Up

Laura Barton

Her mum's got all these porcelain ornaments on the mantelpiece: kittens, boots, puppies, little watering cans and china bells. Every one in its right place. Half past seven and I'm passing the time, mixing them up and switching them round. There's a ballerina where the cherub used to sit, and a basket of flowers that's turned into a swan.

Half an hour I've been here in her mother's dining room with the smell of beeswax and Brasso and the sound of the evening buses outside on the street. And now I've downed three Madeiras from the miniatures in the cabinet, and my mouth feels all warm and sticky and sweet, and I'm picking a hole in one of her doilies. I've almost forgotten why I'm here.

Shelley. She's the most beautiful girl I've ever seen. I used to sit in double maths and just look at the back of her beautiful neck. I'd wait all day for that class, counting down through geography and English lit, through canteen lunch and PE, standing barefoot in that freezing gymnasium, the thought of Shelley Simpson's neck keeping me warm.

When I asked her out she didn't answer for three days. I was so nervous I got a bellyache. We were hanging out by the chippy, me and Paul and Dean, when she turns up with Samantha. And while Samantha's stealing

Deano's chips, Shelley sits down next to me on the wall. She's drinking a Panda Cola, and there's a little arc of cola on her top lip. I keep waiting for her to wipe it off. And while I'm waiting I'm eating my chips, one after another, chip after chip, and then I look down and all the chips are gone.

Shelley looks at me, and she smiles, a big cola-lipped smile, and says, 'You're not going to offer me a chip then?' And my neck goes hot. 'D'you want to go out? With me. Sometime?' I say it quickly, and the words taste of vinegar.

She swings her feet. She's wearing pink sandals that pinch her skin. I lick the salt on my lips, watch her feet, wait. It feels like hours. Then she finishes the last of her cola, hops off the wall and says, 'Hey, Sammy, let's go!' I watch her walking off down the hill, and just before she disappears out of view, she slides her arm into Samantha's and they laugh.

Three days later the telephone rings. It's Samantha. She's got this kind of scruffy voice, and she tells me: 'Shelley says you can take her to the pictures.' I want to whoop and twirl around the hall. I want to waltz down my street and hammer on all the doors. But instead I swallow my smile and try to sound a little nonchalant. 'Oh. Good,' I tell her. And then, because I want to sound a little mature, I add: 'Thanks, Samantha.'

That was three months ago. Now we're going steady. But stuff's all changed since then. Nothing feels the same. We finished school a week ago, and it was like being set free, like the air tasted different, all clean and sweet. I thought to myself it's like I've been waiting, waiting all this time to taste this air. All those years in that classroom, in that fucking shirt and those grey pants with that fucking tie, breathing in all that chalk dust air. Now my dad wants me to get a job in the factory with him, but I think to myself it's just a different uniform, a different dust, you're still counting down the days, counting down the hours till your time's up.

I was in the supermarket the other day, standing in line with a can of beans, coins in the palm of my hand, all sweaty and damp. I was thinking to myself, Is this how it's always going to be? Standing in line – for the supermarket, for the bus, clocking in, clocking out? And I was there in the post office, queuing for some stamps – Deano calls them sticky pictures of the Queen – and I thought, What am I doing here, waiting in line for the throne? I don't have time for all this standing around.

I said to Shelley, 'Let's run away, me and you, let's get married, let's go to London and live in sin.' And she laughed. And I said, 'C'mon Shell, I'm serious.' And she picked her nails and said, 'What about me mum? What will me dad say?' I said, 'Stuff it. It's our time now.' She looked at me and she brushed her hand through my hair. She said, 'Give me some time to think about it.'

Shelley's the first girl I've ever loved. I love the way she smells and the way she feels and the way she tastes of strawberry bubblegum. First time we kissed was round the back of the community centre. She let me put my hand under her jumper, and her skin was so smooth and warm. The next week she let me unbutton her school blouse. She was wearing a bra with little peppermint ducks on it. By the Whitsun holidays I'd seen her knickers. She said we could do it when her mum and dad went away. She said we could do it when we finished our exams. She said next time, next time. But it's been a week now and I'm still waiting.

She stopped wearing the sandals, she stopped listening to The Sweet. We spent all our pocket money on records and hair gel and copies of the *NME*. May bank holiday she pierced my nose with a needle and an ice cube. My mum had a fit. She said, 'Steven, what's happened to you? You're dressing like one of those punks, you're listening to all this horrible music, and you're smoking – don't say you're not because I ran into Mrs Taylor in the baker's and she said she'd seen you in the park. I don't know what's got into you. Is it this girl you've been hanging around with?' She shook her head and straightened my T-shirt. 'You used to be such a sweet boy. You know it doesn't seem five minutes since all you wanted to do was ride your bike and read your comics.' I smiled and I kissed her on the cheek. I said, 'Mum, times change.'

Shelley's dad is in the lounge. He's got the radio on, listening to the football scores. And her mum's in the kitchen, boiling veg. Shelley's upstairs. I can hear her in her bedroom above: the scrape of coat hangers on the rail, the soft thump as she swings shut her wardrobe door. She's got a record on and she's doing a little soft-shoe shuffle while she puts on her lipstick and fixes her hair.

I had one hand in her bra and one hand up her skirt, and I told her I'd wait forever for her, and when I said it I meant it, but now I'm not so sure. There's a show across town tonight at eight, upstairs at the Duke. I've a pair of tickets in my jacket pocket, and everybody's going. But now it's quarter to eight, and even if we run all the way we won't make the start. I'm tired of waiting.

Down the stairs she'll come, all pristine, all immaculate. She's started wearing all this eyeliner and green shadow and she draws in her lips all hard and dark. She looks pretty cool but she never understands that how I like her best is all mussed up, the way she looks on cherry brandy at the end of the night, the way she looks when we come out of the pictures on a Saturday afternoon and she's blinking in the daylight. I call her sometimes and she's been napping and when she comes to the phone, all drowsy and slow, I can picture how she looks, with her eyes half-shut, and her hair all scrawly.

I part the nets, look out on the street. There are kids playing hopscotch, neighbours watering gardens. This summer is a hot one. The grass is yellowing already. Across the street there's a woman sitting out on a garden chair with her dress hoiked up around her knees and she's fanning her face with a magazine while her husband stands belly-out in his vest and opens a can of beer.

I lick my lips. Today is the hottest day I can remember. I changed my T-shirt three times and ran a cold bath. But still, it's like the air is clinging to me, like the day is spoiling for a fight, like something's going to explode. I look at the couple across the street, at the sweat patches under her arms as she lifts her magazine, at the way grey hair is curling out from under his vest and back from his forehead. I wonder how long they've been together, how long they've been living here on this street with all its identical houses; I wonder if they ever have sex anymore, and if when they're going out on a Friday night she still keeps him waiting while she's getting ready and putting on her make-up.

I drop the curtain, push across the dining room, leave the chairs askew and the china rabbits all mixed up. If we go now we might just make it. We might make the gig, we might make tonight, and we might make it out of here, out of her mum and dad's house and out of this street and out of this town. Enough of this standing in line. Enough of this waiting around.

'Shelley?' I shout up the stairs and my mouth is heavy with Madeira.

'Shelley?' A little louder now. Her dad comes out to the hall. 'Everything alright son?' he says. And her mum's there with a pan of steaming cabbage, asking what all the fuss is about. 'Shelley!' I yell from the bottom of my lungs, loud enough that she'll hear me above her record, loud enough that maybe the couple across the street might hear me, might stop their fanning and their supping and wonder what the commotion is.

Shelley's out on the landing, tight jeans, ripped T-shirt, barefoot with her hair half-done. 'What's on fire?' she asks, frowning down at the three of us in the hallway. Her music rushes out through her bedroom door, and the football scores spill out of the lounge and the kitchen smells come flooding through the open door. And in my jacket pocket I can feel the weight of the tickets, and somewhere in my chest I can feel this pressure, like the force of all the wide world out there, waiting. Shelley stares at me.

She has this beautiful face and this beautiful neck, her bra strap slipping down over her shoulder, and the jeans she let me unzip, and those feet that once swung back and forth over the gravel in a pair of pink sandals, and that mouth she has painted but that I have kissed a thousand times and that once wore nothing more than a wet arc of cheap cola. 'Shelley,' I say softly. 'Time's up.'

'Sheena is a Punk Rocker' is an exuberant blast of a song that takes me back to my teenage self, where with black hair and a stripy sweater, a copy of *Times Square* in my VCR, I looked rather like a little Ramona. I saw the Ramones so many times I lost count and they were the first legendary band I ever got to interview for *Sounds*. I still treasure the memory of how cool Joey and Marky were to a starstruck nineteen-year-old hick from the sticks.

Sheena is a Punk Rocker

Cathi Unsworth

I thought it was just going to be another boring Saturday night. Finish work at the guesthouse, put on our glad rags, spike up our hair and spend the next three hours trailing around, waiting for something interesting to happen. That was the way my usual Saturdays went, in the cursed summer of 1984. But this one didn't end up that way. I've often wondered if I actually willed it all to happen, through the malevolence of my own boredom.

I was sixteen then and between two worlds. I'd just left school and would be starting art college in the autumn, to study fashion and get the hell away from nearly everyone I'd been forced to spend the last five years with. Couldn't wait to rid myself of the childish vestiges of school, the small-minded confines of my peer group.

Trouble was, I was still lumbered with Sheena.

Spooky Gemini I've since been called, the sneaky, two-faced good sister/bad sister that my star sign is supposed to represent. I certainly did have a schizo-phrenic feeling towards the girl I'd met in needlework class a year ago, when our school went comprehensive. It was an unnerving time for someone like me, who hardly had any friends anyway, to take in the hundreds of new faces who swarmed into the newly christened Great Yarmouth High.

Kids from the badlands, the hard schools. Kids with skinheads who hotwired the teachers' cars and burned them up across the football pitch; chancy casuals with V-neck waffle jumpers and hands like sticky octopi. Mean skinhead girls with denim skirts and bandy legs; eyes that dared you to look askance so that they could start a fight.

I had already been cultivating my defence against this world that I didn't understand and wanted no part of. If I had known who Jean-Paul Sartre was, I would have fully agreed that Hell is other people, but I hadn't got to art college yet. Instead, I had my older brother's record collection and his teenage leather jacket that he had decorated so painstakingly with white Airfix paint. A picture of an eagle with its wings outstretched, a row of arrows behind its head, a baseball bat clutched in its left claw. Around it, in a circle, block capital letters spelt out the legend: JOHNNY • JOEY • DEE DEE • TOMMY. At the bottom, in block capitals, it said: RAMONES.

It was too big for me but that didn't matter. When I wore it, it felt like a protective shell, like David was still there, with his arms around me. I liked to think I could summon him back by playing his records over and over. Even though they all sounded so strange to me, discordant, weird and angry. The faces on the front covers looked scary too – the black fringes and sunglasses of the Ramones, the ghoulish quiffs and curls of The Cramps, The Clash standing down an alleyway, all sneers and cheekbones. But gradually my ears adapted and I realised that he had left me the greatest gift he could have, this brilliant music.

I had understood the Ramones first, so they were my favourites. I suppose their music always had that pop hook in it, even when they were singing about things like sniffing glue and getting lobotomized. And I sensed a kindness in Joey's voice, he sung more like another girl than a man. As he stared down at me from David's wall, from behind a pair of purple, oval shades, it occurred to me that he was twice the size of the other three. Being only four foot eleven myself, I recognised a fellow freak and from that moment on, Joey kind of merged with David in my brain, became the older brother that was taken away from me in the summer of 1982.

I bought some black hair dye and a pair of crimpers, wore tight black jeans and David's jacket, horrified my already shattered parents and made sure none of those beer boys with wandering hands ever went near me again.

There were a few others like me at my school. We were easy enough to spot and, even though our year was split over three streams, nine forms and twelve subjects, we managed to find each other. Usually in the art room at lunchtime, where we'd sit in a little blackhead circle, drawing pictures and talking about music.

There was Brian Moorcock, aspiring comic book artist; Marc Palmer, who came from London and was obsessed with The Sisters of Mercy; Sally-Ann Pitt, who looked like Siouxsie Sioux and Julian Dean, who modelled himself on Marc Almond.

It wasn't just our hair and clothes that made us different. When I look back now, it's almost laughable the textbook range of our alienation. Brian's family were Mormons, Marc's were Jews, Sally-Ann's were Jehovah's Witnesses. Dean was black and two years away from coming out of the closet, I was a midget with a dead brother. And then Sheena . . . Poor old Sheena had more to hide than any of us.

Sheena had come from Greenacres, the hardest of all the hard schools. She had a reputation, but of that I was blissfully unaware, when she first sat down next to me in needlework and started chatting away like she'd known me all her life.

I wasn't used to such friendliness and it disarmed me. Sheena looked rough, even by the standards of the skinhead girls. Her hair was dyed burgundy, cut into a wedge with steps at the back and a little rat's tail left snaking down her neck. Black eyeliner smudged her inner eye, thick gold across the upper lid; clumps of mascara stuck her lashes together. Her orange foundation did nothing to disguise the patches of acne on her cheeks. Sheena didn't wear a shirt or tie, just a tight-fitting V-neck sweater with an equally skinny pencil skirt and turquoise court shoes, worn down at the heel. As if to make up for the poverty of her uniform, her neck, fingers, ears and left ankle were adorned with gold-plate jewellery. Around her throat, a further ring of love bites, half-covered with toothpaste.

But for all of that, when she said her name was Sheena it invested in my brain a cache of glamour. I didn't realise normal people could be called Sheena. Sheena was one of Joey's New York punk rock names, much too exotic and cool for Yarmouth. Sheena was the girl in my favourite Ramones song.

Kelly Grimmer warned me off when I walked home with her that night. One of my neighbours, Kelly was fifteen-going-on-fifty, a rotund, hen-like replica of her mother, who always knew the gossip on everyone.

'You don't want nothing to do with Sheena Shuckford,' was her advice. 'Seriously, Debbie.' She looked at me solemnly, lowered her voice to a whisper. 'I in't spreading gossip, like, but her mum's a prozzer and an alkie, goes in and out of St Nick's the whole while.'

St Nicholas' Hospital was our local loony bin.

'There's a kid as well, a little brother, so she says,' Kelly continued. 'No sign of a dad anywhere, course. She's had social workers round, police, you name it. You don't want to get involved in that, do you? You'll get a reputation.'

It was those last words that got to me. Kelly might have meant well, but the implication that I would be thought of as a mad slag just for knowing Sheena filled me full of rage.

I kept the warning to myself, and during next week's needlework, made a point of sitting next to Sheena again. After a while, she started telling me about her little brother, Shane. Her eyes lit up when she described him. He was three years old and she had it all memorised, when he'd said his first word, taken his first step, even the less endearing milestones of his potty training.

'I look after him I do,' she said, snappling open the locket on one of the many chains around her neck. It was in the shape of a love heart, and inside was a blurry picture of a little boy with a head of white curls. 'He's gorgeous, in't he?'

Emotions broke inside me like waves. I had to look away, out of the window.

I felt her hand on my arm. 'What's up, Debs?' There was real concern in her voice, even though she hardly knew me.

'I used to have a brother,' I said eventually.

'Used to?'

I looked back at her worried face, took a huge deep breath.

'Yeah,' I said, forcing a smile, thinking of Joey Ramone. Too tough to cry. 'He would have liked you, Sheena.' I meant it too.

On an impulse, I invited her home to listen to David's records. She went mental when she heard the Ramones, loved the song about Sheena. I suddenly felt able to speak about what had happened to my brother for the first time. Maybe it was because I felt sorry for her, maybe it was just the love she had for her own sibling that made it seem OK. But after that, we were stuck like glue and I didn't care what Kelly Grimmer and her morality police thought about it.

Sheena reciprocated my interest by changing her appearance. First it was the rat's tail that got snipped off. Then it was the crimpers, half-inched from Woolies. The gold jewellery was replaced by studded wristbands, all except the locket with Shane's picture, which maintained an incongruous presence at all times. She got herself a leather jacket and some biker's boots, tight black jeans and a mohair jumper. By the end of term she had finished it all off by dying her hair black. We looked like Da Sisters Ramone.

She came round mine a lot to listen to records and talk. Sometimes she brought Shane with her. He was a quiet kid, with staring grey eyes, who sucked on a dummy and clasped a tatty beanbag Piglet. I don't think I ever heard him cry. Not even the extremities of punk rock, goth or psychobilly could upset him. No wonder Sheena loved him so much.

I was never invited back to hers, though, and I didn't ask why, just nodded when Sheena told me that her mum wasn't well enough. If she didn't fetch him straight from home, she would always go back early to look after Shane. Sheena told me about the social workers, that much of Kelly's story was true. She was terrified they might come back and take him away.

'It's not Mum's fault,' she would say. 'They don't understand, she just in't well. And I can look after him all right myself, can't I?'

I never doubted it. I just wondered how she fitted in the boys she was supposed to be so fond of, where all those love bites came from.

Then came the summer job at the guesthouse. Sheena had been working there for the past two years already, and when one of the other girls dropped out she got me a job. We had to be in at seven to do the breakfasts, then chambermaid the rooms until twelve. Back again at five for the evening meals. On Saturdays it was changeover day and we had to work for longer, making beds and scrubbing toilets. On Sundays and bank holidays, we got time and a half, a whopping £1.50 an hour.

I managed to rake in about forty quid a week, which meant I could go up Norwich on Saturdays with Marc and Sally-Ann or Brian and Julian and blow the lot on another pile of vinyl from Backs Records.

Sheena never came with me. It wasn't so much that she was wary of my other friends, although she always went silent in their presence. It was more like she actually seemed physically afraid of leaving Yarmouth, being too far away from Shane. Or maybe it was her mother who put the frighteners on her. I had an idea that at home, Sheena was little more than a slave.

The only time she got to go out was on Saturday nights, after she had come home to deposit her week's wages, then met me back at mine to dress up. Only Sheena wouldn't want to go in to town, where I could meet the others in The Oakwood, the weirdos' pub, where we could get away with being served. Sheena always wanted to trail up and down the sea front, spending what was left of her money on the 'musies or the rides at the Pleasure Beach. Stuff that was for kids, I thought, and after a while, it started to bore me rigid. I began to tire of her company and even looked forward to the start of term.

Kelly Grimmer was right. When it came to the crunch, I didn't really want to get involved.

Back at school, I worked like mad to get my portfolio together to try for art college. I spent more time in the art room, less time with Sheena. But she was hardly ever at school by then anyway.

Sheena was hauled up by the truant officer the day I got into art college. I saw her standing outside the headmaster's office just as I was coming back, triumphant in the knowledge that I had avoided another two years of torture at sixth form. I will never forget her wild eyes, the way she was feverishly scratching at her arms.

'Debs,' she whispered, 'they're going to kick me out.'

I tried to look sympathetic, but in truth I was irritated that she was ruining my good feeling.

'They caught me working up the Front,' she said, her eyes boring holes into me. 'I don't know what the fuck to do now. They . . .'

But the headmaster's door opened and they ordered her inside and I never found out the rest. I wondered what 'working down the Front' meant and assumed that it was a job she had got in one of the arcades or the caffs. Then I got on with feeling smug about art college.

Sheena would have faded out of my life as quickly as she'd come into it if it weren't for that guesthouse. A couple of months after she got expelled, she turned up at the school gates. She had stopped looking like a punk by then. Her hair was back in its wedge, bleached blonde. She had on tight stonewashed jeans and a green US Air Force bomber jacket.

'Mrs Beckett wants to know if you'll start again next Saturday,' she asked. 'For the Easter bank holiday.' Her eyes were pleading and I noticed a mauve shadow underneath the left one, where the concealer had worn off. 'It'd be really good if you could,' she added. 'I've missed you, Debs.'

I felt a rush of guilt.

'Yeah, course,' I heard myself say.

We walked home together and she was full of chatter. How things had turned out for the best, that now she didn't have to go to school or bother with taking her exams she could look after Shane full time. Which was just as well as her mum had been in hospital again. But she was out now and things were going to be fine. She was looking forwards to spending another summer with me. She was sorry she hadn't really kept in touch, but you know, she'd been so busy . . .

My heart sank but I kept smiling, as I continued to do throughout the rest of the summer. By the time we'd reached August, that smile was wearing thin. The more desperate Sheena became to try and tell me what was really going on, the more I brushed her hints aside. My one concession was the interminable Saturday nights down the sea front, which I bore with gritted teeth, the words to 'I Wanna Be Sedated' churning ironically through my snotty teenage mind.

Until that night.

Sheena was banging all of her loose change into Pac Man in Circus Circus, while I lounged against a fruit machine, trying to ignore the infernal electronic whoops and whistles of the packed arcade. As I glanced across at her, lost in concentration, pumping the little gearstick up and down in time to the chewing gum in her mouth, I offered up a silent prayer.

'Please, someone interesting come and deliver me. Anything's got to be better than this . . . '

As if the heavens had suddenly interceded, Sheena ran out of money. We wandered out onto Marine Parade, wondering what to do next. Sheena began to hint about hitting the Pleasure Beach and I started to grind my teeth.

Then I spotted deliverance. Brian and Julian were heading our way, toting carrier bags full of cans.

'What you two up to?' asked Brian. 'Want to come to a party?'

'Sounds good,' I said, seizing the opportunity before Sheena could open her mouth. 'Whose is it?'

'These friends of Marc's from The Oakwood,' Brian said. 'They've got a flat on St Peter's Road. You probably know some of them, a couple of them go to art college.'

Brian had made it through too. He was going to be starting graphics in September. This was obviously meant to be, our first opening into the art college social whirl.

'Great,' I said. But Sheena just stood there, looking miserable.

'I don't know, Debs,' she said, her bottom lip

jutting out as if she was going to cry. It made me see red and I would have probably snapped at her if Julian hadn't stepped in.

'It's OK, they said we could bring our mates. They're a good lot, and we've got enough beer, don't worry about that. I reckon it'll be a real laugh.'

Julian had a gentle way about him that instantly defused tension. Sheena looked at him warily, but I could tell she was pleased to be spoken to this way.

'Are you sure?' she said.

'Course I am, girl.' He winked. 'You stick with your Uncle Julian.' And he threaded his arm through hers, led the way down Trafalgar Road, away from the Front, and down Nelson Road Central to the corner of St Peter's Road. By the time we got there, we were all chattering happily and now that I'd got my own way, I started to feel magnanimous towards Sheena again.

The door was opened by a tall guy with black curly hair and a pair of purple granny glasses. He looked just like Joey Ramone.

He ushered us through with a fatherly air. 'I'm Shaun,' he introduced himself, 'and down here it's greebos corner.' He swept his arm around the room where an assortment of bikers sat on a battered leather sofa.

'Through there's the kitchen where you can leave your beer. Then upstairs, there's goths and punks in the front room, beer boys to the right, hippies in the back right and elitists in the back left. Make yourselves at home!'

I thought he was joking, but no: the flat was a cornucopia of degenerate youth culture, and just as our host had promised, they all had their very own room. The hippies were listening to The Doors under a purple lightbulb, in a room draped with Indian print fabrics. The beer boys – all two of them – were Rod Stewart lookalikes singing along to their hero. We didn't quite dare to check out the 'elitists' and headed instead for where we thought all our friends would be – the punks and goths room.

It was like stepping into heaven, with a soundtrack by The Damned. All around sat the beautiful creatures of the night, their hair spiked and coloured, their outfits incredible. Sally-Ann was there, talking to a girl who looked even more like Siouxsie than she did, with flame red streaks at the front of her towering black birds' nest hair. Marc was talking to a big punk rocker with a black and pink mohican, several nose rings and a missing front tooth.

The drinks went round and we all got talking. The music got better and better. Someone put on the Ramones and me and Sheena just looked at each other, put our cans down and started to pogo. Sheena was a punk rocker again, her face alive with delight as we shouted out the words, grabbing hold of each other's shoulders and bouncing round the room.

'Oh my God,' she said as the song ended. 'I'm about to wet myself! Gotta go to the lavs!' Shrieking with laughter, she made for the door.

I scrambled for my beer, necked it fast. The room was starting to reel.

Then the punk rocker came up beside me and said: 'I hope you don't mind me asking, but are you Debbie Jones? It's just that I recognised that jacket . . .'

Everything became suddenly still.

'Yeah,' I whispered. 'Did you know David?'

Of course he would have done, I realised, he's

about the same age as David would have been and David used to look like that, before . . .

'Yeah,' said the punk rocker, offering me his hand. For all his fearsome appearance, his eyes were gentle. 'Chris Bull,' he said. 'But call me Bully. I used to be good mates with Davey. We used to go to gigs together, hitched all round the place. It was just so weird seeing that jacket again, I had to come and talk to you.'

My mouth opened and closed but nothing came out.

'See this,' Bully shrugged off his own leather, showed me the back of it. Below the word DISCHARGE he had painted a picture of a dove caught on the blade of a knife.

'We painted them jackets on the same night, same tin of Airfix.'

'It's beautiful,' I said, tears in my eyes. I couldn't believe it.

'Shaun,' Bully called across the room, 'Karl, come here a minute. This is Davey's sister.' In a moment, the Joey Ramone look-alike and another punk rocker with orange hair were standing at my side.

Joey, who was really Shaun, checked the back of my jacket.

'Of course,' he said. 'Davey's leather. You're a chip off the old block in't you?'

I didn't know whether to laugh or cry, so I chose the former. Encouraged, Shaun, Bully and Karl started telling me stories of their exploits with David, hitching across the country, seeing the Sex Pistols play at West Runton, following the Ramones, getting a job as roadies for The Damned. They were just like my brother, so funny and interesting.

'We was lost in Croydon once,' Shaun said, 'and we

didn't have a lift, so we went to get some chips and try and find the train station. Trouble was, we were so pissed we totally lost our bearings. Davey wanted a slash, so he goes into this garden where there's a big old bush to hide behind. He starts squirting and suddenly all the lights go on, the front door opens and this bloke's standing there going: "What the hell are you doing?" Quick as a flash, right, Davey goes: "Midnight Gardener, come round for a spot check. Your plants needed a water and I've noticed that your Wisteria could do with a bit of a prune, want me to do that an' all?"'

I started laughing.

'Bloke just stands there, open mouth, can't believe it,' Shaun continued. 'Davey zips up, walks towards the Wisteria and the bloke goes: "No, it's all right thank you, don't want to take up any more of your time," and shuts the door. Could you believe it? Davey's pissing in his garden and the bloke's thanking him for it. But that was just like him. He never lost his cool.'

My laughter got harder, verging on the hysterical. Then, as if someone else had taken charge of my tongue, I heard myself say:

'So why weren't any of you at David's funeral?'

That cut the laughter stone dead. They all looked at each other and then Bully took hold of my hand and said: 'I don't think your folks wanted us there, Debbie. It was too much of a reminder for them, you can't blame them . . . '

'Reminder of what?' I didn't understand. 'Of all the good times he had? Why is that wrong? I would have met you before, it would have been better . . . '

'Well,' Bully looked round at his friends, 'it weren't us was it? It was that Carol. Only she was a punk too.'

'Carol?'

'This dodgy boiler he started seeing,' Karl took over the story. 'Bird from Norwich, we met her down the Jacquard one night and Davey, old Mr Cool, just flipped. Started going up there all the while, we didn't hardly see him no more. Said he wanted to marry her . . . '

My mind was reeling. I didn't know any of this.

'Then she just like dumped him. He wouldn't tell us why or what it was about and he stopped coming out. That's when he . . . '

'Shaved his head and joined the army,' I finished the sentence for him. Cold chills blew through me. It was like I'd found David again, just to lose him a second later. 'Got himself blown to bits on Goose Green.'

'I'm sorry,' Bully pulled me into an embrace and I clung onto him as the revelations tumbled through my mind like a row of dominoes falling.

What happened next is still like some mad dream. Every time I try and bring it back it fractures and distorts into a million different variations.

One minute I was crying against Bully's chest, breathing in the smell of his leather and tasting the salty tears on my tongue. The next came the noise of screaming.

I had forgotten about Sheena. Hadn't wondered why she had taken so long in the lavs, just assumed she'd got talking to someone, like you do at parties. Other people pieced it together afterwards, in the cold light of dawn, down at the cop shop. Then at the inquest, in court and all over the local papers, when suddenly everybody wanted to get involved in the sordid details of Sheena's life.

Sheena had been waiting for the toilet to come

free, outside the elitist room, when someone had come out of there and she'd peered inside the door to see the very person she most wanted to avoid. The reason why she would never come with me down The Oakwood, the reason she was shy of my weirdo friends.

She started banging on the bathroom door.

'Let me in! Let me in!'

But nobody had and this fella had seen her, got to his feet, started walking towards her. He was a big, hard old fucker called Raymond Bowen, who went around in a great-coat and had waves of grey hair and piercing grey eyes. The reason that he was holding court in the elitist room was because he had all the drugs.

Not just the spliff and whiz that people at this party were taking. Harder drugs, like the stuff she got for her mother. And Sheena was late on her payments.

He came up to her with a nasty smile; just as the goth who'd been throwing up in the lavs came stumbling out. Sheena tried to dodge past him, get into there and bolt the door, but of course, he was much bigger and stronger than she was. He locked them both in there. And then, whispering threats of the worse things to come, he did to her what he had done to her before, when she was twelve years old and her mother was short of cash.

He raped her over the toilet seat. Sheena's mouth opened to scream but no sound came out. It wasn't as if she hadn't been used to her body being abused. It had been that way ever since she'd hit puberty, the only way she could help her mother and keep hold of Shane. It was just that he was the one who had started it all.

He was Shane's father. Her son's father.

Just as my memories were caving in on me,

Sheena's were on her. And it was worse, much worse for Sheena. When he had finished with her, Bowen bashed her head against the cistern and walked out. The pain of the impact started the scream.

Sheena staggered out onto the landing. She didn't know where she was or who she was any more. She just couldn't stop the scream, the scream that had been welling up inside her for all her brutal, horrible life. She had her trousers round her ankles and blood was running down the insides of her legs, and down her face, from her freshly broken nose.

People came running towards her. One of the beer boys got there first. She was standing right on the top of the stairs, wobbling, screaming. He reached out a hand to grab her and she shied away from it, fell backwards down the stairs.

Landed on her head and broke her neck.

The screaming stopped.

If only I hadn't been bored that Saturday night. If only I had gone to the Pleasure Beach like Sheena wanted. It wasn't much to ask of a friend, was it? That she could steal back some moments of her lost childhood on 'musics and fun fair rides, pretend to be normal for one night a week.

That Shane could have a mother who loved him, instead of being sent into care and God knows where that left him. God knows if he even remembers her now.

But I still do. Even though all I have left of her is all I have left of my brother: a song by the Ramones. A song bursting with adolescent joy that brings back those last few moments when she was young, happy and alive. And I hope that, wherever her spirit went, Sheena is a punk rocker now.

'Another Girl, Another Planet' is a fizzy rush of a pop song and it's arguable whether it even is a punk song. For one thing, it has one of the best guitar solos I've ever heard, which I used to rewind on my tape player, over and over. Punk is probably associated with less proficiency and more brevity, but I see it as a direct mode of self-expression that obliterates everything in its path with a brazen abandon. This song contains that spirit. Punk inspires other people to create, which is why I wanted to write something for this book.

Another Girl, Another Planet

Paul Smith

We catch trains so that we can enter each other's world. Another long journey; re-entry to her atmosphere. The conductor had a teddy-boy quiff, where the dark hair behind each ear bore the trace of his fingers, creating slick horizontal ditches on his skull. The curled front of his hairdo was fluffy and precarious as he leaned over to sign my ticket. He squiggled his signature using a stubby little biro like those you used to get in bingo halls and betting shops. He was wearing a dated, utilitarian, navy-blue suit that made him look like an extra from *Jailhouse Rock* and he moved about the train from seat to seat, at ease with his job and his environment. As he walked back into his compartment, some kids who had table seats switched on their phones and the tinny barrage of compressed, high-tempo music began again. Opposite me, a young woman changed into a pair of trainers, peeling off her flat office shoes delicately. Her whole demeanor changed and her body slackened. She looked up to see if anyone had noticed and then closed her eyes.

'You've been staring through that window for five whole minutes.'

'I know.'

'Well, where's the fire?'

'Just looking at the name of that hotel. The one that's lit up in big red letters.'

'You don't need to describe it to me. I see it every day; every morning. Ho hum.'

'Mmmmh.'

It was like this more often than not. She probed and I shuffled. Back and forth without any real momentum. In time, her body would shrink and fade in colour until she was transparent and susceptible. Her demeanor remained hardened and she seemed to anticipate the leaks in any suggestion; anything less than what she perceived to be genuine was hounded down. Maybe she was right to be that way.

Looking down, I took a photograph of the car park from the window. The white grids were perfectly spaced so I waited until the cars that came and went seemed to form a regular pattern. As usual she was waiting for me to leave the flat as I dithered.

'Come on, I'm always waiting for you!' I said.

'Shut up, you,' she replied, exasperated but laughing.

A daily routine was already established. The green tiles of the vestibule glistened and our voices would ricochet around the stairwell as we checked her mailbox. The lift was often broken in her apartment block. When the lift was working it was slow and we would pose in the mirrored wall as we descended. I would fix my hat and she would suck her cheeks inwards whilst titling her head upwards. Sometimes I would pick her up in a big bear-hug and we'd wobble about before the doors opened. Then we would smirk our way out past whoever was waiting into the muted light of the city centre.

We walked without purpose.

'It's like there's two of you: the one I see when you're with me and the one who does whatever you do when you're not with me.'

I always went on the defensive when that sort of comment arrived. They came unexpectedly after a period of contemplation, or late at night when we huddled beneath her thin sheets. Invariably, they came before I was about to go away again. I would agonise over what to say and how to deliver it, but that method only seemed to make things worse, looking like I was stalling over saying some unutterable home truth; the dreadful delay of someone who's thirsty to get something off their chest despite the unwanted consequences. This time, though, a watershed had been reached and instead of the usual anxiety I found myself sinking into the pillow, unable to stop my eyes from shutting.

Some hours later I turned the sheets over and leaned out of the bed gently so I didn't wake myself up too much. The hard skin on my bare feet brushed along the laminated floor in the dark hallway. I kept my eyes scrunched up, half-shut, as I pulled the cord and the bathroom light came on. As I moved towards the toilet, I stood on something sharp. I reached down on the floor to pick up a hair clip before studying it in unnecessary depth. The ends were grazed and worn; grey where the paint had been lost. I placed it on the side of the bath. The bathroom was bare apart from a few products dotted around; a white, blank space, free of mementoes or baggage. Some soapy rings stained the porcelain surfaces. There was no towel to dry my hands.

Weeks later, I found myself worn out in a hotel lobby, much calmer than I had been for a long time. I got into my room and threw my bag on the bed as the door clunked behind me. I was in darkness and I realised I would have to go back to the doorway and fumble around for the keycard holder to activate the room's power. I tried to imagine what it must look like from outside: another golden cube appearing in a broken grid; another stranger appearing three seconds later to draw the single curtain.

I laid out my vital bathing accompaniments, including a book that I'd been reading for ages with little hope of completion, and began to run a bath. However hard I tried not to get water on the books I read in the bath, they always ended up with a grey drop spoiling the page or a shriveled corner that I would later find as I reopened the book. As usual, the bath was too hot and, as usual, I had no intention of waiting so I tentatively lowered myself in using the handrail. The clear water's surface came to meet the ridge of skin that ran around my leg from the tight elastic of my discarded socks. At the very moment when the two lines met, I thought of an eclipse.

A long pause followed as I hovered above the inevitable. After a large intake of breath, my backside breached the stillness of the water. The rest of my body hurriedly descended in an easy movement that belied the surge of activity underneath my skin, which reacted to star-shaped heat rushes by covering itself in a flush. I stopped myself reaching for the cold tap, reasoning that the experience must be doing me some good.

Eventually, I lurched forward until I was sitting upright staring down at my immersed feet, strangely pale and distorted. No one can reach me here, I thought. My open mouth was dripping from my bottom lip. A peculiar mix of tap water and saliva steadily dropped into the bath, creating a fertile trail that spiralled and whisked. Such a pretty little mess.

Back on a train, I wondered less about what had gone wrong than how it had begun. She was distant now, in every sense; several months soon turned into a year. Through the large windows, a familiar, evenly paced tapestry unravelled. Ever changing, ever-the-same embankments collided with the fringe of various housing estates; somehow dated and timeless. Young, stunted trees struggling to make progress in blanched, open grassland suddenly gave way to brambles and evergreen bushes spilling over each other, alongside the tracks.

On the scruffy, plastic table lay the same book I'd meant to finish all those months ago. Her photograph was the bookmark. I picked it out as I stalled on the last few pages in a familiar ritual meant to prolong my enjoyment and memory of a story. Under scrutiny, the picture revealed little of the feelings once attached to it with such intensity. Its totemic quality was so reduced that it came as a shock. I closed the book, losing my place, and tried to recapture some memory or essence that would compensate for this emotional amnesia. How much of my knowledge about her was formed in those first, impressionable days? Did it leave me blind to subsequent events? That initial grapple left me floored, dazed even, but now my eyes were studying her smile as if to bore beneath the printed surface. Momentarily, a local train pulled alongside, on parallel tracks, its four lurching carriages brightly lit. As the tracks diverged, the rear of the train came into view, with a digital display spelling out 'Airport' in crude, illuminated cubes. A girl wearing a winter hat briefly returned my curious gaze; the only one to make eye-contact amongst the bodies pressed against the glass doors of the opposite train; another girl, another planet.

> I remember sitting glued to Annie Nightingale's *Sunday Request Show*, I'd sit in my bedroom with the lights off and a candle burning waiting to see what music she might play that I'd never heard before. I was thirteen when she played New York Dolls' 'Personality Crisis', it seemed so alive and exciting and then on the same show Patti Smith Group's 'Dancing Barefoot'. Those songs just seemed to speak to me and informed my life from then on.

Dancing Barefoot

Lois Wilson

You are talking and I watch your mouth moving, your lips forming every word, and I know I am staring but I have long since stopped hearing what you are saying to me because I see only him and I hear only him and I am lost in the past, and have forgotten why we are both here because it seems so unreal now. The record that you have just been playing on the Dansette stops and the whirring of the turntable gradually comes to a halt as the arm makes its precarious way back to its rest. 'I loved Patti Smith,' you say as 'Elegie', the last track from *Horses* clicks off. 'She was always an inspiration. I mean everything about her . . . ' and you are away and talking and I am back in the sixth form and reading out the lyrics to 'Piss Factory' in English class and making my own pathetic stabs at writing Beat poetry in a notebook covered in badly cut out pictures of the New York Dolls and I have pulled my black jumper down way past my knees and I awkwardly pull at my dyed black long hair and chew at my nails, as I watch the clock's minute hand tick round so agonisingly slow until the time comes and I can go and see him again.

My tiny cassette player is taping everything you say as you pick another record out of the pile to play me and I nervously check that the spools are turning round and the machine is gently humming and the red light is on so it is recording and I will be able to write about you later. And you have so very much to say and you are so very interesting and your stories are so full of excitement and enthusiasm and I feel overwhelmed by your experiences and your knowledge, you keep talking and now you are telling me about Joy Division and how amazing they were. And I am back in my Manchester and he and I are putting sheets of tinfoil on our walls, sticking them up with Blu-Tack, because somehow this makes our one room look like The Factory to us and the steam from the kettle from which we have made our soup from powder is leaving droplets of water on the shiny surface as it turns to condensation and we trace them with our fingers as they make their rivers and run down and we warm our hands around the cups. We are excited because we will go and see Nico play that night and even though the Velvet Underground are long gone and Nico is only on stage to fix her habit we will hold hands and our fingers will wind around each other and we will think that the whole world is there for the taking because we are watching this wondrous woman with a voice that freezes our very souls who used to know Andy Warhol and Lou Reed and John Cale. And we go home and sit on our bed and as he idly strums his guitar we will talk about situationism and Marx and the 1968 Paris Riots and the Prague Spring and how much we are in love with each other and we don't realise just how there are teenagers all over the country having similar conversations thinking they too will make things happen and that they too are so very different from their classmates. And he will rub his black spit mascara eyes as the night draws to a close and the sun starts to rise and he will push back his kohl hair and he will smile sweetly, his brown eyes searching for recognition and understanding and he will place in my hands a battered copy of Camus' *L'Etranger* which he bought for 10p earlier in the day but had forgotten until now that he had bought it for me.

And as I sit here in your studio I wonder now if we were nothing more than a cliché and you tell me about your plans for your new album and how all the different ideas are feeding into it and I am in awe of your motivation and your drive and your joy for just creating and your eyes sparkle and flicker and you really have changed people's lives. And it was punk that inspired you, you tell me, you were right in the thick of it, you got to see every band, saw the Pistols and Buzzcocks at the Lesser Free Trade Hall in 1976, Iggy Pop at the Apollo in '77, Subway Sect, The Fall . . . the list forms like a who's who and I can't imagine what it must have been like to be you, to have been there at every important gig, and then to be famous from seventeen, to have been so good at playing the guitar and so good at songwriting, and so good at articulating the emotion welling up inside, to be worshipped every time you stepped on stage and every time you stepped off it. To never really know who liked you for you and who liked you for what you do, and it must get lonely not really knowing even who you are sometimes, just a person to be photographed for a poster to be stuck on someone's wall, to be interviewed by a stranger about what you feel inside and have to make an instant connection with them and hope that they will write something nice about you in their magazine.

And as you play 'Dancing Barefoot' to me I see his mum slowing walking up our path, his dad supporting her as her feet stumble to get their footing and as I look from our window I know something is wrong and I feel an instantaneous panic and I remember my words, an argument, a silly argument about nothing but I had said that I hated him and the world stopped turning at that moment, it just stopped, everything ground to a terrifying halt and I stood giddy, swaying slightly and she burst into tears on our doorstep and I felt the cold air on my face and my heart pounding and pounding as if it would burst from my chest and I was not even aware that the high-pitched scream that was deafening me was coming out of my mouth. And the last time I had heard that record was at his funeral twenty years ago and here today you are telling me it was the record that probably inspired you most to make music.

There are some people who are truly great and some who never get the chance to see.

In memory of Andy Moore.

"The Buzzcocks were formed by Pete Shelley and Howard Devoto after the two met at the University of Bolton in 1975. During this time Shelley lived for a while on Radcliffe Road, Bolton, where he wrote songs and played music in the cellar. He was engaged for a time to Hilary Collins, a fellow student. The breakup with Hilary was highly traumatic but this experience gave birth to some of his first groundbreaking work and was perhaps the inspiration for the notorious song 'Ever Fallen in Love'. I chose this song because I have, as I guess we all have, fallen in love with a wrong one and the lyrics of this song sum up this state of madness and desperation perfectly. It reminds me of a time in my 20s when I lived so precariously with skate-punks on nothing but love and a whim and a prayer. I took my experience, sliced it with this song and came up with this utter punk fiction."

Ever Fallen in Love With Someone (you Shouldn't've)

Salena Godden

Joe lived in our building. He would come knocking at any time of the day or night for aborrowing of something, borrowing meaning a-taking and never giving back, even denying he'd come and nicked it in the first place. This could be your TV or your typewriter, your frying pan or even your toothbrush. Joe had a knack of taking objects you were in the middle of using yourself. He'd come and take your pillow from underneath your dreaming head whilst you slept if he could.

Joe always said, 'If the devil's getting them in, then make mine a double, the first one's always free!'

I knew the devil wasn't to be trusted. In fact, as far as I was concerned, the devil went by the name of Joe and funnily enough Joe was a very popular man. Even now, remembering him, I have to admit I get goose bumps, even though I am in another world and this is all so far away and long ago.

There was no denying it: Joe was very attractive and magnetic too. He had a way about him that made girls boisterous and fizzy. Around Joe, girls were keen to prove that they could urinate standing up, drink bottles of cheap vodka straight and walk on their hands in short skirts. Girls were never ladies around that devil Joe, that was for sure.

I was barely seventeen and I was intolerably in love. My friend Hilary Collins was seeing Pete Shelley and I would tag along so I could ogle at Pete's mate Howard Devoto. For me, Howard was unapproachable. He was older and cooler, he was intense, often lost in deep thought, distracted by his words and music, or so I assumed. It was clearly obvious that he was going to be a legend and I adored him. Of course he barely knew I was alive. I was this awkward geek, an excruciatingly shy girl who had only just left home, but for those months, at that first year at college, I followed them around like a lovesick puppy. I was in cloud cuckoo land.

I shared a studio with Hilary in a red-brick building, an abandoned factory on the edge of the canal. Hilary was a year or two older than me and she was the only person I ever talked to about my secrets. During the first year we became very close; she treated me like her little sister and I really looked up to her. Our building was full of students, wannabe artists and musicians and it was illegal to live there. In the summer it was hot and dusty and the milk soured. In the winter it was bitterly cold. It was overrun with spiders and mice all year around. But we took comfort in the mice, if there were mice scurrying about we figured there couldn't be rats.

The winters were harsh. We'd scout skips and break into building yards for wood, we'd burn anything we found, old cupboards and chairs. We'd huddle up under blankets at night and sit around talking, smoking and drinking, rubbing our hands around the old wood burner to keep warm – we always smelled of bonfires. On those bitter nights the gas rings on the cooker were kept on all the time (none of us paid any utility bills) but nothing was any match for the howling wind licking through the holes in the walls and the gaps in the coal-dust blackened windows.

There was no bathroom or running hot water. We'd boil pots of water and strip wash in a tin bath in front of the fire. I remember those early days with a sad fondness, like once when Hilary and I got quite drunk and we bathed in our army boots. We took it in turns to sit in the tin bath to shrink our jeans, our boots over the edge, wearing cowboy hats, smoking cigars and laughing. We were like *Butch Cassidy and The Sundance Kid*. Hilary and I were inseparable then and I loved her – perhaps I mean the other kind of love, and more than a sister. I would have done absolutely anything for her that was for sure and she knew it. That night we slept in the same bed to keep warm. There was a fizz of electricity and a heat between us. We laughed it off nervously, then, when she turned her back to me I put my arms around her and held her. We were like two warm spoons and when I could finally fall asleep I remember dreaming about her all night.

Everything was recycled out of necessity and everything was nicked, but it was exciting. Being a teenager in love will see you through almost anything. This rebellious and scrounged up life was during the dawn of punk. Sure, they were messy and wild times, but I remember starting most days by pissing in a bucket and cutting the blue mould off old bread to make it alright to toast. Sometimes Pete and Howard would come to ours. We'd bunk off and hang out to the soundtrack of rain dripping in buckets around the place. Something about that feeling, getting stoned and floating with the sound of drumming rain on plastic corrugated roofs, resonates and remains with me for life.

I remember that building was full of characters. There was an old poet who lived downstairs. He was always talking to us about the beats and Ginsberg, he was friendly to us all and gave us spare teabags or cigarette papers. There were these brothers who were art students from Dublin. They had parties that lasted for days – things got smashed, the walls were a mess of graffiti, but funnily enough, it never looked any worse than it did before, and the stairs always stank of urine. There was a Japanese fashion student who lived on boiled cabbage broth and knitted jumpers out of human hair. We had a go-go dancer and a painter who lived next door, and about once a month or so they'd have huge fights and his clothes and paintbrushes would be thrown out of the window into the courtyard below. My favourites though were Birdman and his girlfriend at the other end of the corridor. They were a sweet couple but Birdman was often sick, he was getting thinner and thinner, but you never asked questions. Oddest of all though were the people that arrived from nowhere and came to stay. People would just show up in that building and hang around for a month or so, like the blonde New Yorker, Nancy.

Now Joe always acted like he had money. He'd slip a mention of some royalty cheque and tell you his tab would get the drinks. He told us he had a record deal in America. We'd all seen Joe's seven-inch vinyl: it was a white label, there was no writing or picture on it. He was a singer in a band back in New York. Joe seemed well connected, and he regaled us with tales of touring and he reeled off the names of people from famous bands he'd played with at places like CBGB and The Bowery Ballroom like they were personal friends of his.

'Just put it on my tab babe,' Joe would say.

We'd laugh and someone would holler across the pub.

'Well if the devil is getting them in, make mine a double!'

I'd watch Joe sidle up to the landlord and tell him he'd come and sort it out next week. Or more than likely, he'd leech some cash from one of his girls, like Nancy, to pay for it all, like she was a sport about such things, and he'd tell her he'd sort her out later, which of course he wouldn't – at least not with money.

Joe always had a girl making a fool of herself over him. They were often posh girls trying some life on the wrong side of the tracks. He was never faithful – fidelity was not in his language – but each girl thought she was the one to tame him, to be his special lady. Hilary and I had the misfortune of hearing him delight in embellishing the details. He liked to show them off to us, and his eyes would glitter as he told us the names he'd given them. For example, there was a girl he called 'The Screamer', who loved him to mock-rape her in the park nearby, and 'Plastic Bag Lady', who liked him to urinate all over her. When he told us these dirty stories Hilary giggled, I looked away and Joe laughed at me and cracked his fizzed-up can of lager at my face.

I recall one morning when Nancy knocked on our door. She said Joe told her to come and introduce herself properly. I could tell Hilary thought she was cool when she started swearing more than usual. I thought Nancy was brash and rude, and she smoked like a professional. She had filthy bleached hair and black nails. She made the New York scene sound so wild with her rasping voice and guttural language. I remember we drank instant coffee and cheap whiskey out of pint glasses as Joe had borrowed all our mugs. I also remember Hilary and Nancy really hitting it off and I felt a bit jealous. After they had gone to the pub together leaving me behind, it transpired that it was all a ruse and Nancy had been carefully ejected by Joe because he saw the car of 'The Duchess' parking out front. How the boys all laughed about that one, because 'The Duchess' was apparently funding Joe's solo album, or so he said. It was like Joe's hands were sticky with all the sweets, his fingerprints were left everywhere and with such obviousness it reeled people in. As long as Joe had the majority vote there was no fighting it. He was Castro, it was for the people's good, but no matter how you weighed it up it was a kind of dictatorship.

Gossip was like a soupy grease in that building, you'd slip in it and it was hard to wash off. You knew who'd got paid because you'd hear the laughter, smell the chicken roasting and they'd have their own fags for a change. It was a fish bowl and the walls were paper thin. You knew people's highs and lows, when they had work and when they were off the rails.

I remember a warm summery day when we were sharing out boxes of strawberries that had got knocked off. Some of them were squashed but mostly they were just over-ripe. Flies circled us, we had pink sticky fingertips, and we talked about Joe, you know, how he'd told someone one story and someone else another version and when you put the pieces all together they just didn't add up. We laughed about it, I remember, Hilary and me and the girls all really laughing. Then the rumours about Nancy came up. The go-go dancer said she'd probably gone back to New York. Hilary said that Nancy was with some guitarist in London, but all of us speculated that there was something funny about it. The fact was that she had come into our lives for a few weeks and then disappeared with half of her things left behind and with money owed to Birdman and Joe. She had left a bag of dirty, smelly clothes in our place and had not come back for it. After a while Hilary started wearing her clothes.

Howard once gave me a plectrum. I also remember at one party I lent him my black eyeliner and when he gave it back to me I treasured it because he'd used it. I'd take it to gigs in case he ever wanted to borrow it again. When Hilary got engaged to Pete she'd keep things there at his and at our space too. Sometimes I'd go over to Radcliffe Road and watch Howard, Pete and the band jamming and rehearsing in the cellar. Hilary and I were die hard fans and we went to all the early Buzzcocks gigs.

Meanwhile, down the hall I saw Birdman getting sick and thin. We all knew he was scoring through Joe. I could see for myself that anything to do with Joe would end in tears, anything done to death is death. So one day, Joe knocked on our door and Hilary let him in. Looking back, in retrospect, I suppose she wanted to dissipate the myths, as if to say she could handle the likes of Joe and that Joe was no big deal. I also guess he charmed her into it, he had that persuasive way with girls. She took her tokens and got prepared for the ride of a lifetime. Much later she told me that after that first time, she vomited until she thought she would do her guts some damage.

At the time, of course, I didn't know about any of this. The truth is, when I came home that evening things seemed normal. In the weeks that followed Hilary and I partied and went to see gigs as usual. I didn't know the signs, she kept it secret at first. It took such a long time for me to clock it, to notice she wasn't being herself, her eyes were glazed and pinned. She quit going to classes and when I thought she was at Pete's she was creeping up to see Joe. We stopped hanging out so much together, I hardly saw her, I felt like she was avoiding me.

Then a part of me in the story ends there. It was painful to see her like that, to see her like that around Joe. We had one big fight about it, but she told me I was jealous and to mind my own business. Then Hilary gave me a note to give Pete at college, but I never saw him or Howard to speak to again. It's like we all drifted after that and Pete and Howard and the band were doing bigger gigs in Manchester and London. Around that same time, Birdman told me he'd heard a rumour that Nancy had been fighting for her life on suicide watch, and I reckoned it was only a matter of time until Hilary slipped into those shoes as well. I decided to pack up and leave Hilary there, in that place with Joe and the spiders and the mice.

Now, I distinctly remember that morning as I walked away from that building. It was the shortest day of the year, it was a bright blue-skied December day and there was that crisp nip in the air. I had packed my few belongings into a bag and I was walking along the canal. I began searching in my pockets for my matches to light a cigarette and it was then when I found the folded letter in my pocket. In Hilary's scrawl she'd written the words '*Pete . . . have you ever fallen in love with someone you shouldn't've?*' I'd heard that Pete and Howard were down in London, but I folded it up and posted it through the door at Radcliffe Road on my way to the train station.

When I was a kid on the remote west coast of Canada, punk happened 6,000 miles away from me, but I felt part of it nonetheless. Punk made me move to London as soon as I could, even though I arrived years too late. Public Image was a logical, if perverse, step for the ex-Sex Pistol; they made records to be harangued by.

Public Image

Kate Pullinger

My wife Ruthie and I have become a double act. We have a routine. When we are with other people we have a stock of stories that we tell. We even have our own catch phrases.

Last Friday we were at some friends' for dinner. Our friends, Jenny and Anwar, have twin girls around the same age as our boy; the kids were off in another room, whacking each other over the head with the controls for the game console. There was another couple there as well, people we had never met before; they'd left their kids at home with a babysitter. The evening progressed, we had a few drinks and ate a bit, though not a lot; Anwar is one of those men who fancies himself as a great cook but, in fact, everything he makes is either undercooked or just plain weird tasting. He thinks not using salt means he's into healthy eating; he won't even put salt on the table. It tries my patience. Anyway, we had a few more drinks and got onto the subject of our friend Dave, a fellow everyone seems to think is an International Man of Mystery just because he has a lot of money.

'He seems like a nice guy,' said Jenny.

'Oh he's very nice,' said Ruth, 'he is very sweet.'

'Except when he's drunk,' I added.

'Oh yeah,' said Ruth, 'then he turns into the *Daily Mail*.'

Ba-da-boom. Everyone laughed.

The truth was we'd used this line before when we'd been asked about Dave. I can't remember which of us said it first, but from then on it became part of our routine. Whenever Dave came up in conversation, which was often – people who are not rich are always curious about people who are – we'd trot that line out, reliably. Then we'd embark on our anecdote about the time Dave and Ruth had a stand-up row over democracy. Tonight was no different than any other night; Ruthie told the story while I sat back and chuckled encouragingly.

Ruth said, ' "People," Dave announced, "are too stupid for democracy." '

That night, in the restaurant with Dave, Ruth and I had looked at each other across the table, amazed. Dave had made the transition from Mild-Mannered Liberal to Raging Rightwing Demagogue before our very eyes, without going into the phone booth to get into his costume first. 'What do you mean?' Ruth asked.

At the time I shook my head at her but she ignored me.

'People don't put any thought into how they vote,' Dave said. 'They just pick whoever they like the look of. These days they pick whoever is more famous, whoever has the best story. We should leave voting to an educated elite.'

And so our anecdote continued. Our friends and acquaintances were always interested in this routine. I guess that's how it goes when you develop a double act; you figure out what material works, and what doesn't. You occasionally try something brand-new, but mostly you stick to the tried and tested. The story about the row with Dave would often lead to another row with whomever we told it to; it seems that there's a lot of people who are transformed from Mild-Mannered Liberal to Raging Rightwing Demagogue once they've had a bit too much to drink.

Friday night was no different. This time Jenny took exception to my wife's ironic tone. Her voice was shrill. 'Dave's got a point, don't you think, Ruthie?'

'Ah,' said Ruth, 'no.'

'No?'

'No,' replied Ruth.

I attempted to intervene. 'Ladies,' I said, but that was a mistake; calling certain women 'Ladies' winds them up more than calling certain men 'Gents' ever could.

'Shut up, Dick,' said Jenny.

This came as a shock. Jenny had never told me to shut up before. I don't think I'd ever heard her tell anyone to shut up, no matter how much she had had to drink. And – this was the bigger shock, in fact – she had called me 'Dick'.

My father named me Richard; it's a name that is easy to dislike. It wasn't his name, nor his father's, nor any other relative of ours – I don't know why he gave it to me. The shortened forms of Richard are all awful: Rich, Rick, Richie, and the execrable, excruciating, gender-specific, Dick. For a while at university I tried to get my friends to call me Chard – I thought it sounded cool, like charred or maybe even Che – but that didn't go too well; Chard rapidly became Pilchard. That got shortened to Pil, which was okay because at the time we were all listening to records made by PiL, or Public Image Ltd, the band Johnny Rotten tried to make work after the Sex Pistols. But, like the band, the name Pil didn't stick. They only called me that when they were thinking about it and my friends and I weren't all that big on thinking, despite the fact that we were at university. My name is Richard; there is no escape.

I had to say something to Jenny. I had to retaliate. Now, I'm not a retaliating kind of guy. If you insult me, chances are I'll laugh, then go away to seethe in private. But Jenny couldn't tell me to shut up AND call me Dick AND get away with it. I sat back and listened to the ongoing conversation which had, thankfully, moved on from who should be allowed to vote. I felt tired; I yawned and stretched and closed my eyes for a moment, to gather strength. But when I opened my eyes and looked around the table once again, I realised I despised my friends. There's nothing like a dinner party to make you despise your friends. I resolved that Ruth and I would stop sharing our double act anecdote about Dave.

Ruth doesn't like her name either, though I am fond of it. 'Ruth,' she barks, 'Ruth. It's so plain. It's so Bibley.' In our house, 'Bibley' is not a good thing. I escaped from my father because he's a monster; Ruth escaped from hers because he was way too Bibley. 'He loved the Good Book so much,' she'd say, 'he'd use it as a weapon.' And she meant this literally – her dad used to hit her with the family Bible whenever he felt she had transgressed the creed. As she got older, naturally, this became more frequent. She used to listen to PiL as well and for her the anger in those records was real, as though that band had a hotline to her mashed-up and outraged soul.

When our boy was born we gave him the perfect name. It suits him so well just saying it makes me feel happy.

I had stopped paying attention to the dinner party and the conversation; why are conversations at dinner parties always so stupid? The mix of friends and once-met acquaintances is lethal; it means you can never really talk about anything. You end up discussing celebrities.

I had another drink. Anwar had got out the thirty-year-old sherry; it was like alcoholic crème caramel, smooth and burnt tasting. You were only supposed to have one small glass of it, but I poured myself another when no one was looking; they were too busy talking about Victoria Beckham. I interrupted: 'I liked PiL,' I said. 'They were the musical equivalent to complaining about your parents – loud, irritable, ominous, and profoundly whiney.'

Everyone turned toward me. Ruthie gave me a look so mixed up with alarm and pleasure that I almost laughed out loud. She said, 'I remember all the words.' And it's true, Ruthie does remember all the words to all the songs; it's an alternately annoying and reassuring character trait. We could make this part of our double act, in fact, Ruthie and her uncanny memory for lyrics. She began to sing the song 'Public Image'. Ruthie is a good mimic; she caught the snide nasal tone of the song perfectly.

I smiled at my wife. I think Johnny Rotten meant those words for Malcolm McLaren but that didn't matter; like with all the best songs the words are really meant for Ruthie and me. We rose from the dinner table at the same time, said our goodbyes, and collected the boy from where he was watching age-inappropriate DVDS with the twins.

In the car, which Ruthie drove because I'd had too much to drink, I said, 'Being middle-aged isn't all it's made out to be.'

Ruthie laughed.

'Let's give dinner parties a rest for a while,' I continued.

My wife nodded. 'OK.'

There's a Pennie Smith Clash photograph, grainy black and white, taken on a stairwell somewhere between stencilled shirts and tiger stripe camouflage trousers. In it, Joe Strummer wears a wide-brimmed trilby and a polka dot bandana, Topper has on a white tux, Paul Simonon is in black, smoking, and Mick Jones is part Ted, part Mississippi riverboat gambler.

Career Opportunities

Lee Bullman

He'd been Terry Razor since way back. Since mid-winter 1958, when the knot of street-corner Teds in Paisley told him he couldn't join, told him he was too young. Since they'd narrowed their eyes beneath messy oil-slick pompadours and turned up velvet collars on long jackets. Since they'd shook their heads slowly at him and cracked gum like they saw heroes do in the movies.

'On ya go, ya wee shite, on ya go . . .'

The girls were with them, Jacquie and Tina, with the kohl eyes and beehives, sweaters, pencil skirts, scarves. Lighting up corners of the night with long pulls on lipstick-smeared filter tips. They'd smiled down at him and run red chipped nails through his hair. He'd fixed his eyes on the scuffed toes of their pointed shoes, skimmed the sole of his own shoe across the surface of a puddle, watched the light break and ripple and decided there and then that he'd form his own gang.

He recruited from the local kids his own age, the eleven and twelve year olds he knew from school and the nearby streets and tenements. The Teddy Razors were born, knee-high delinquents with their hair worn back, carrying blades as a non-negotiable requirement of membership. The Teds got back in touch. They wanted someone to climb through the back window of a shop, to let them in so they could rob the place of cigarettes. Terry told them no.

He left school rather than finished, then went through to Glasgow and caught the train to London. He hit the outskirts first, fifteen years old and staying with a relative he barely knew out in Burnt Oak, taking soul-destroying, mind-numbing, piss factory jobs twirling telephone cable and maintaining milk floats. At the soda siphon factory they put him on the production line, where he had to hit four buttons, in sequence, every fifty seconds.

He got fired a lot.

He looked around the magnet city. The strongest pull emanated from its centre, from the streets around Soho Square. He found a wonderland of murky desire and barely suppressed violence, a dark pantomime played out beneath the twitch and buzz of neon signs soundtracked by Telecasters playing shapes from Burt Weedon books and blues records and slot machine payouts in arcades where boys his own age were. Sex shops, strip clubs, speakeasies and Formica casinos all played musical premises with one another in the square mile, swapping location daily, weekly.

Suddenly it was a beautiful summer.

In a boozer close to Chinatown he met three brothers from Aberdeen and George, the mod from Wapping, in his milk bottle glasses beating a rhythm on the pub table. All four men made their living from the clubs, or *vice clubs*, as the *News of the World* had started calling them. There were about fifty like them working

Soho on any given night, five times as many women. When Terry asked what were the chances of getting some work, George filled him in, talking double-time, bombed on pills, pupils huge. Terry smiled, listened.

'There's three main ways you can earn down here outside of outright thievery. You need to know how to Mumble, the Corridor, and how to set up a projector . . . Mumbling's the most important, you can't do nothing without it . . .'

The Mumble was the simplest scam they operated.

All it required was the ability to convince Joe Public that a garden of fleshy delights awaited him the very moment he parted with hard-earned pounds, shillings and pence, and a doorway to do it from,

'Find out what the punter's after, then offer it to 'em . . . Offer them strip clubs, sex clubs, floorshows . . . Blue films, pink films, red films, any colour they want . . . Promise 'em girls, Terry, promise them black girls, white girls, girls in twos and threes, girls who can satiate and satisfy the deep-seated desires they didn't even know they had. Mumble tales of boudoirs filled with wonderful, wanton, willing women . . . Then take 'em round to one of the flats in Greek Street.'

The girls they took them round to, usually found on the first or second floor past the MODEL sign above a bookies or a bakery, paid commission on every client acquired on their behalf by the Mumblers. Most of the girls kept maids who handled their business. Terry liked them all.

George kept talking. His tennis shirt was made of breathable cotton, small laurel wreath at the chest. His eyes narrowed and his voice dropped, like he was passing on a secret.

'And if you ever want to get shot of a punter, it's easy. Tell 'em you're gonna take 'em somewhere special, guide them through a crowd, theatre-goers at the end of a performance

maybe . . . a pub calling time. Then all you do is choose your moment and stop dead. Stand still while the mark, mind racing fast as his Hush Puppies'll carry it, keeps on walking. Five steps is all it takes, when there are five steps between you, reverse, nearest side street, alleyway . . .'

There was an art to the Mumble. It was all in the delivery, the performance of the danger that the punter was looking for. It was using vague phrases that left blanks for the would-be John to fill with his own sickness. They watched the men they Mumbled drool and stutter, they watched beads of sweat form at their top lips and shirt collars. Terry took to it quickly and was always good, the Scottish accent helped.

The Corridor ran between Lisle Street and Gerard Street, Chinatown, near Wardour Street. An architectural anomaly thrown up between the two streets, it was basically an alleyway with a door at each end. Terry and a couple of his crew would man the door at the Lisle Street end and wait for a mark. They'd know him immediately by the cheap suit and whiff of nerves and purpose. They'd Mumble him the promise of the girls who flitted and played in his half-drunk imagination and he'd pay, willingly, gratefully, and they'd let him into the dim corridor, pointing to the door at its far end and telling him that he could get greedy and wild. Once they had stepped out into China Town's busiest thoroughfare, disappointed punters made their way straight back around to the Lisle Street door, which was by now locked and unattended. The Corridor could pull in a monkey, on a good night.

If a punter returned later, being bothersome, making demands, then a swift right to the bridge of the nose usually sent them back on their merry way. They had short, vicious fights in the doorways of Soho, no drawn out brawls. Terry only ever stood a chance if the other guy had thrown the first punch, kick, or glass. He never won a fight he started.

Maltese Joe operated out of an office on Berwick Street from where, amongst other things, he administered rents for the people who really ran Soho. The Maltese were renowned in the area. Tales illustrating their propensity to resort to sensational violence were legion and told in corners of pubs across the city. For a while they ensured that if anyone did ever try to loosen their grip on vice, they only tried it once.

Joe was the man to see for those who imagined themselves short-let West End movie moguls. The premises were let out strictly on a night at a time basis with cash paid to Joe at the end of the evening's business, no excuses. For your money you got the use of a room floored with mis-matched squares of worn carpet and fading rugs, a rag-tag selection of chairs facing a grubby sheet tacked onto a wall, the whole scene illuminated by a single red bulb. Facing the sheet at the other end of the room atop an unsteady barstool stood a battered black and silver Keystone 16 millimetre film projector.

Joe didn't provide any movies, so they went to a shop close to Leicester Square station that got hardcore stag reels flown in from Copenhagen. The films were illegal on the streets of London, too explicit, too close to the knuckle and the inner thigh and the small of the back and the nape of the neck.

Terry would load up the projector, feed film through spindles and watch as the dirty mac brigade paid their money and filed in and shuffled to their seats and waited for the show to start.

The projectors overheated, every night, midway through *Alison Baba and the Forty Thieves* or *The Plumber Calls* or *The Naked World of June Taylor*. The film would burn out and dissolve right before their eyes. From the back of the room Terry watched in awe as the frames of sad-eyed women in fishnets and heels with hollow smiles and faint bruises suddenly became flickering volcanic explosions of hot red and orange edged by burnt black, grainy monochrome peeps of spread legs, willing mouths, and whiplash cruelty. Psychedelic porno burnout just as the first tabs of acid were about to hit Soho streets. Refunds were not given.

Terry had always rhymed with poetry, writing, reciting, since he'd heard it first at school. Lately he'd started coming up with these long sinuous ropes of automatic fantasy he could unfurl on request for the working girls and shoplifters he breakfasted with occasionally at the New Piccadilly. Sometimes, as a kind of party piece, he'd write a poem with his eyes closed, on a folded out napkin.

When Donovan released *Sunshine Superman,* Terry set up stereo speakers facing out onto Wardour Street, three doors along from The Marquee, and played the 45 on repeat, letting the words and music drift over to nearby Carnaby Street, where London was apparently swinging.

One night he's working Lisle Street with Tony. To their right is an Italian restaurant, below them and to their left, at basement level, is a strip club. Tony disappears into the club for a drink. He's gone a while, comes out a changed man.

'I'm in love. I just met her Terry. Down there. I'm in love . . .'

In the early hours Banky showes up. He is selling hoisted engagement rings, got five with him, gold bands with a single solitaire diamond. Tony buys one of the rings, pockets it.

The next night Terry's was working with Tony again, on Wardour Street. Tony goes off for a while to see his girl, comes back . . .

'She's a man.'

Terry looks at the ground. What *do* you say?

'It's still love though . . .'

The next week they were gone, the Mumbler and the dancing girl left Soho together in a cab. Terry never saw them again.

As night hardened into morning the supply of punters would dry up and Terry and whoever he was with would head off to the gambling clubs over in Covent Garden, then for a drink at the Kemble.

The Kemble's Head was on Bow Street, close to the Magistrates' Court and populated by those who had some business in there, policemen from Westminster's Vice Squad or further afield, or the accused they would be facing. A lot of business was done in the Kemble as the sun coughed up fully over central London. Familiar faces in huddles with cops, buying drinks, passing bribes and the names of those they wanted arrested. Working girls and Mumblers sat nursing double Johnny Walker reds as they waited side by side to appear before the magistrate, a crisp ten pound note on hand ready to pay the inevitable fine that meant they were free to go and start all over again. Terry appeared there a few times, charged with running unlicensed cinemas.

For a time before he moved into the flat above the cinema on Rupert Street, once he'd left the Kemble decent rest and recuperation was bought for the price of a ticket on the Circle Line. A corner seat with the collar of his Crombie turned up as the train rocked him to sleep making its way through Gloucester Road and Tower Hill, Baker Street and Paddington, round and around, round and around.

With the arrival of the 1970s his nights grew in scope. More and more he found himself on the King's Road meeting these snooty but nice old money types who thrilled at how close he could get them to the centre of the action in Soho without getting their wings burnt. He met them in the Speakeasy, at the parties and balls he found himself invited to over in the Royal Borough of Kensington and Chelsea.

He took them to Pam's bar, above one of the clubs on Wardour Street, his favourite spot, and pointed out the local celebrities as his audience of the almost aristocracy gasped and guffawed at Eartha Kitt and Shirley Bassey. Wanted men stood rounds at the bar for Chief Inspectors and off-duty CID, last rounds were bought before James Albert Keane, resident of the Isle of Dogs, handed himself in for the sub-post office in Cheam.

The King's Road types liked having him around. He could *get* stuff and started to score drugs for them, pills, pot, whatever they desired, and sell it to them at a mark-up sufficient to ensure that he could leave the Mumble, the Corridor and the Blue Film Parlours behind.

In the end, though, Soho was inescapable. He started selling to people who were making money in the pop business, managers and promoters, drummers and songwriters, he drank with them in Denmark Street, still a stomping ground for those with an eye permanently peeled for the next big thing. He started working on the fringes of the music industry, thinking that it wasn't so different from running a film parlour or Mumbling. It was all showbiz.

He took an office on Denmark Street, he resurrected his old name and started to introduce himself as Terry Razor.

There was a guy called Malcolm who Terry was seeing around more and more. Malcolm dressed like the Teds had back in Paisley, gold tie, blue drape, brothel creepers, pomade quiff. He sold clothes with his girlfriend from their shop on the King's Road. By the mid-70s Malcolm had begun looking for a group. Once he'd found his boys, with some luck and a fair wind behind them then who knows, he said, they might even be as big as The Bay City Rollers.

Once in a Lifetime (or The Last Slaves)

Alan Donohoe

'What one generation finds ridiculous, the next accepts; and the third shudders when it looks back on what the first did.' – Peter Singer, Bridging the Gap.

And you might find yourself, walking along on the cobbled streets of an old port town, past your old school and the park where only a few years ago you would play. The smell of flowers and grass pass, to be replaced by fresh bread and food from the bakers and restaurants. The sun shines down and you pass familiar faces and places, girls are shopping and grown men ride past on important business.

Continuing down the street, passing a shadowed doorway that Mother would drag you past as a child, you recall how she would grasp your hand and mutter how you must never, never look inside. Today you walk down and enter a courtyard cut off from the warm sunshine by high old walls – all damp and cold. Muffled noises echo round the square where ivy and mould cover the walls. Shivering, slowly you enter the shadows.

In one window there's a large group of figures, seemingly trapped in a room and unable to move.

They look ill and exhausted. Shocked and confused, you wonder what is happening here, just metres away from the normal world, in this hellish, hidden place. After thinking for a moment, you tap on the window to get their attention. Some spin round. Terrified they begin to scream. 'Shit! Shit! Shit!' You run to the other side of the courtyard to catch your breath and cool down and wait for them to stop.

Sliding along the wall, peering around a corner, you see there are others being lead down to the ships. Heads down, prodded if they walk too slow. You feel disgusted and you feel pity for these victims. If one falls the others are forced to continue, stepping on the fallen who are beaten till they move on or till they stop moving at all. You just left a world where girls were shopping for the latest clothes and shoes, while men worry if their job is as good as their friends.' A blanket of denial. A thin veneer of civility stretched over this hidden brutal reality.

Head now filled with nothing, hearing the sounds of a struggle and a desperate, chilling scream. You're not in yourself now. Your body moves to another window, one hidden furthest from the world you so comfortably resided in before today. Although dreading to see what is inside this room you still look automatically, blankly inside. A man is struggling over a figure lying on the ground. He picks up a knife and straddles the figure, who tries to struggle under him, weakly pushing out his leg to stand but fails. Some say, there is a hierarchy and we stand at the top. The knife comes in quickly under his chin. A final scream is uttered but stops when the man slices through his neck, a sick gurgling sound replaces the scream as blood splashes to the ground. The victim stops kicking after a few moments, you feel sick and your head is spinning. So many thoughts are thrown up like a mess.

You sprint from the courtyard down the tunnel into the street and the light. The world is, just as you left it, undisturbed by what you've seen.

You run to a café. There are people you know there. People older than you. You have to tell them. They have to do something. You tell them what you have seen, of those trapped in the room and the screaming and the group being shipped and the suffering and the killing. They stop you.

They already know and are not shocked. There's no problem. They have no problem. 'You're being too sensitive.' OBJECTIFICATION.

The world is falling in on you. How can everyone around – close friends, family – 'Water! Get some water!' – good, decent people, live with this brutality, engaging in it, revelling in it – fainting, I think.' – in this revolting brutality that has just awakened and consumed you?

It's objectification that turns black people into slaves . . . *and you might find yourself sliding down into the seat* . . . its objectification that leads women to be raped . . . *beside the man talking about his recent promotion as a product designer and the girl with the Zara shopping bag* . . . it's objectification that turns any beings into mere things . . . *both now eating a part of the animal's leg who was killed in front of you.*

Listening to The Slits conjures up visions of West London at a very particular moment in the 70s. I wasn't there in the physical terrain of bombsites, abandoned terraces and motorway flyovers but my imagination was fuelled with grainy footage of riots, heat waves and punk rock. A version of London was constructed in my mind, filtering the areas around Ladbroke Grove, Latimer Road and Portobello through a lens of desire and mythology. I have written about the Westway a lot; about my walks underneath it and the people I've met on the way. For many years it seemed that that the 70s scene was irretrievably foreign. In the 90s and 2000s, with gentrification sweeping away the rubble and empty houses, those earlier times of West London as playground, as porous city of the imagination became crystallised in folklore and memory, almost completely beyond reach. Now though there's a sense that those times are returning in a mutated form, that squatting and improvisation will return to the area by necessity as markets crash and house prices plummet. By the time I arrived in London in the early 90s the flashpoints of creativity and insurrection had shifted eastwards and the landscape of my own desires was mapped out between Camden town and Hackney Wick.

Liebe And Romanze

Laura Oldfield Ford

Eyes pressed to the window I yearned for the first ragged boundaries of Edgware, that liminal zone where motorway flyovers arched across dilapidated precincts. The slow arduousness of that coach journey seemed to illuminate the desire. Stranded up North I saw our first encounter played out in such vivid clarity, a warren of corridors, the gently undulating terrain of the Fleet valley, it was the most alive sequence. We roamed through blocks, subways and abandoned arcades, he had that New York punk look, black hair and an eye tattooed on his hand like a Masonic talisman.

I'd spent ages getting done up, red dress, hair a backcombed mess, eyes all dazzling with emerald glitter. The narrow paths above the Heath were suffused with the scent of jasmine. I passed the row of big squats we used to live in and slipped through an avenue of corrugated iron. There were strings of coloured lights, bonfires and caravans. A last tumble down narrow steps and I emerged in a dusty yard where stacks of speaker cabs sent tremors of dub and punk rock reverberating across the ground.

They were all there. I had seen so much slip by, people disappearing one by one into the obscure morass of faded photographs and yellowed letters but here in the pink haze of twilight was the whole crew, unchanged sitting on crates and barrels drinking Boss cider. I wondered with a shock jolt how it had happened and how I must appear to them.

I saw him later on with a group of the old crowd from Hackney. There were broken tables and chairs, old household furniture thrown out and reclaimed under the elderflower trees. He was from Leeds, in this band that were like Gang Of Four fused with Voivod. You should have seen him, black hair, royal blue eyes, sometimes glinting indigo in that sanguine light of dusk. His eyes played mesmerising tricks with me, the dark lashes, the intricacies of desire shuttling between us. Shall we go for a walk? He had a bottle of red wine, good stuff too. The light was a soft mauve through the trees, the meshes of suggestion formed a canopy above us.

I wanted his kisses so much when they came, the memory traces of his beautiful spectral face, on and on, through fragrant elderflower corridors, endless proliferating tunnels, through the banks of soft violets.

There was a door, dark green, the paint was peeling, and he pushed it open leading me into a rambling overgrown garden. There was buddleia and hollyhocks, snapdragons and honeysuckle. Come with me. Coaxing, gently pushing, on through the tangle of briars and wild roses. I followed him up a flight of stone steps to a hallway cluttered with cases and boxes. The floor was black and white and spanned out in checkerboard formations. All around were convex mirrors, the kind you get on the underground. It must have had five flights of stairs with stained glass windows on every half landing; he led me right to the top, to an attic room. The curtains were drawn casting a pink glow over a brass bed and dark furniture; it looked like an old rented room from '70s London.

I'm living here at the moment. Why don't you come and stay with me?

I could hear noise downstairs.

There was a battered tape recorder playing all these songs from the old days, Mudhoney, Fugazi, Melvins, and some drunken singing, there were about 15 people living here he said, mostly French, some Canadian.

He pulled me towards him, hands around my waist, thumbs digging into the pelvis, it all seemed so fraught, the eye on his hand duplicating in the wall of mirrors.

This was one of the enchanted places that slipped out of sight, only to emerge and reconfigure elsewhere. In the alleyway, another undoing encounter, climbing the fence. You sure? Yeah, the greying nets, a slight flutter, the grime and mess. A room with falling wallpaper, faded roses, mildew and moss, he cut his arm getting through the window. You sure? There were numerous portals, fluctuating and reversible like a Baroque ceiling, lenses opening onto other realms. I didn't even know him, but that's how it worked, a last grasp, a last attempt to go back. Then there would be a pause, but I had never known a full stop. In my life, there was always an adjunct, a sequel, a little bit more.

The coach stopped at Golders Green station. I began a slow drift with a hip flask of rum to the Heath. The ancient pathways were hazy with smoke as I dropped down to the glowing windows of the Vale of Health. I searched in the winter murk for the traveller site behind corrugated iron, briars and hawthorn.

The covert symbols of chance encounters were visible there. The city had become cinema, signs oscillated and shimmered. I found scattered rice and hearts chalked on stone, markers forging future pathways. The city was a character in flux, vivid and psychoactive. Surveying London from Parliament Hill, it sprawled under a canopy of ruptures and livid blooms. All our boltholes, rooftops and hidden yards, they were mine to find again.

We had been circling around each other for months. He was there, on the periphery, sometimes on the radio, in the papers. Beneath January skies the heath was patched up with a sombre palette of greys and ambers, ivy spanned the crumbling red brick of the bridge. I retreated there to think, to become lost and tranquil. In the Vale of Health there was a small tarpaulin city, it reached in sketchy lines from the traveller site. There were strings of coloured lights and bonfires burning under low trees.

We had walked on the heath together, looking out over a London smarting and smouldering but still there. As quickly as the skyline altered with glassy futuristic towers so it reverted as one by one they were rendered jagged smoking ruins. The building in London had ceased years ago, then the patching and mending stopped and finally commerce and capital abandoned it altogether and left for the band around the M25.

Up on the heath in our little hideouts, mossy walls and hidden paths, we had wandered together planning our escape. Now I went out again, on another search of the city.

As soon as I spied The Stag on the corner of Fleet Road I sensed I'd crossed an imperceptible boundary that had taken me beyond the grasp of affluent Hampstead and into a realm of inebriation and anxiety. In the violet light of the beer garden I watch the snarl-ups of rejection, the smashed pint pots and upturned chairs. I paused to call on a lost acquaintance in Palgrave House and pushed through amusement arcade kitsch, tainted nets and falling draylon. A cat in the communal launderette dozed between geranium pots.

The place was a nest of junkies, the dank pain of boredom spanned the threshold. I hadn't been here for nine years but everything was the same, even the scorched teaspoon on the gas fire was still there. It was a zone operating out of time, stuck in a dim yellow glow, possibly 1986. There was a sense of the frayed last days of Goth, the determined traces of patchouli incense and dark red velvet blocking out the light. A broken TV cast phosphorescent light over the ashtrays, rizlas and torn up cigarettes. It was a cocoon of mourning, a grotto occupied when the idea of a life had been abandoned. I drifted out of those flats with that dislocated feeling you get when you emerge from a matinee.

Queens Crescent, nexus of knife crime, a flashing matrix of Sheffield steel. There was a scene outside William Hill, a tableau of immanence. In the searing July heat, homeless blokes were sitting in a cluster waiting for personal issue payments.

The street market was suspended somewhere between 1968 and 1981, and I sensed my darling there, on the corner of Baset Street and Allcroft Road. I searched the brickwork with dusty fingertips for the first Sex Pistols graffiti of 1976. He was here then, and possibly now, we drifted in circles around each other.

Desire raced all over me, little shivers of pleasure, bursts of erratic joy from shoulders to finger tips Japanese animation, white explosions of gunfire, '80s synthesiser soundtracks.

In the fabric of the architecture I uncovered traces and palimpsests, the poly-temporality of the city. On the corner of Herbert Street I traced unintelligible glyphs on peeling stucco, a tally of condemned men. This was the yearning for the mythical homeland, the invisible cord.

I gravitated as always to the late-night linctus apothacaries. I wished I could get a grip on this thing, but it kept turning up, impossible to walk in a straight line. I was floating through the vistas, De Quincey scag meanderings, dizziness, inner ear malfunction. He was here, a phantom, haunting the walkways and court-yards, I sensed his presence in the gentle coaxing of the terraces.

I glanced across at Bulls Pizza And Bagels, the diamond patterns in bleached pastel colours sent me forcefully back to 1982. I felt sick, drawn in, chamber after chamber, worlds unfolding like a computer game. Someone shouted 'Wotcha!' And I thought how I'd never heard that beyond the heterotopia of the cinema. Here in the burnt out shopping arcades, the boarded up precincts, I sensed a certain truth, that a new space might be opened up. Amidst the labyrinthine corridors, walkways and roundels there might be a rupturing of this collective amnesia.

Serious assault 18th august. 2 males involved in stabbing incident. We are appealing for witnesses, can you help us?

Arcade game violence seeping through the cracks, threshold disintegrating.

The Man of Aran pub. I felt alright in there with the flashing fruities, slashed up leather and red pillars. It carried an air of seedy abandonment, no one cared that I was too wasted to speak on shoddy scag derivatives. John Legend on the jukey.

I felt the cold scuttling sensation of cathexis, Proustian flashbacks, something about walking around Highbury Barn at four in the morning, a drowning guilt, the loss of someone I loved. If I could pierce this soft, soft grey. An enclave steeped in nostalgia for the Crimean war, Inkerman, Alma, this pub stands as a ghostly marker, that nothing is ever learned, the charge of the light brigade, the idiocy of the officer class... it all returns, over and over. Smearing red lipstick in the fluorescent glare of the mirror I thought maybe I'm looking better now, after a drink, less wrecked.

Sex crime 1984.

Weightlifting, video shacks with Jackie Chan fixations . . . the tattooed eye on the left hand, the trace of the eye drawn in the condensation on the café window.

And all the guilt I harboured, all the shame, the walk around Highbury with so much hanging in the balance, the tyranny of choice and the crashing cruelty of desire, it was all locked into that one anodyne song.

Song ends, bag opens, rummage, find money, put it on again.

Beyond the pub lay the corridors of industrial ruins. Crumbling pathways opened up between derelict '50s factories. Dislocated bontempi rhythms came cascading from an abandoned coffee grinding factory, *Jesus loves me! He will stay, Close beside me all the way; He's prepared a home for me, And one day His face I'll see*. We crawled beneath cables and graffiti-lit walls. There was a massive squat party in one of the industrial units with all these speaker cabs stacked up in pyramids.

Townships of portakabins spanned the railway arches like a Gustave Doré etching. I dropped through a trapdoor and descended into an appropriation of imperialist fanfare, Throbbing Gristle broadcast loud.

Lured by curiosity and desire, I played the game for the sake of playing, endless inescapable configurations, Homo Ludens with a diseased mind. The second time, round the back of Queen's Crescent, he wouldn't let me go without my phone number. We were under a bridge in Arctic Street, he pushed me hard against a wall emblazoned with THE JAM and FLUX OF PINK INDIANS. We broke into a prefab cabin where a yellow strip light showed up the dusty remnants of an adhoc canteen, a ruptured dartboard and faded copies of the *Sun* strewn across the floor.

We followed the path of the Fleet and watched London cascading, cinematic and charged, rows of pastel mansions slipping and tilting into the ravine. When we got to Inverness Street there were hordes of screechers and brawlers, a real demented din. We weaved through alleyways and takeaway miasmas, dodging packs of drugged-up kids and salacious chancers. Canal Collective Squat was now derelict but still buzzing and seething under heaps of detritus and giant hogweed. There were punks necking cider outside the front, a little den of mayhem, doors leading to musty corridors and someone playing The Membranes through broken windows. The town, in the heart of the heatwave, had become a maze of carnivalesque loopiness.

Join with the friends of kebba 'dobo' jobe who was killed last Saturday – 15 May 2004 – while being arrested by police.

My eyes were done up emerald green to match the high heels. Camden Lock, the Glasshouse 1984, there was a gig down here, Crass and Flux Of Pink Indians, futurist nihilistic noise unleashed under a canopy of glitter balls and balloons. The street was suffused with a hazy pink light; I watched the figures slip into a concealed doorway, a backward glance signalled the beginning of another slow search of the city.

I imagined the pale skin, the badly tattooed eye on the left hand, I would recognise him anywhere, that swagger, the slender frame. The memory traces of his beautiful spectral face, on and on.

That night, the hands around my waist, thumbs digging into the pelvis, it all seemed so fraught, the eye on his hand duplicating in the wall of mirrors. I trusted we would find each other again, I wouldn't tell him my name, I let him guess, refusing to write my number on the proffered hand.

Royal College Street was quiet and strangely depopulated. 'The French Poets Paul Verlaine and Arthur Rimbaud lived here May-July 1873'. Their rooms lurk behind a façade of peeling stucco and schizoid eruptions of buddleia. This is how the days were, solitary, walking through the city communing with the revenants. I paused before the ghostly carapace of The Falcon. It lay slumped beneath a patina of dust and lichen, festooned with dead ivy and scorched hanging baskets.

I squeezed through splintered hardboard and broke in round the back. There were smashed windows and blackboards announcing 'Foster and Kronenburg £2 a pint' in that swirly writing that's supposed to look like chalk. I sat on a mildewed banquette smoking a cigarette willing it to come alive again, dreaming of it packed out with juvenile delinquents in Crombies, borstal dots and cherry reds. I brushed masonry dust off the jukebox and let the ghostly strains of Cockney Rejects ricochet around.

The red glow of the basement lit up the narrow stairwell. I emerged in a tableau of mirrored alcoves, tiled walls and a population of déclassé deviants on smack. I was sent reeling onto the dance floor by a load of crew off the estate, drinking fizzy piss, dancing on little diamonds of broken glass. Pulled back to the velvet banquettes, I turned sharp, half fell, a tattooed eye reflected in the mirrors, on and on, indigo and red lights pulsating in the heat haze and sweat. His eyes were royal blue, violet in that sanguine light.

The soft musings of melancholy gave way to fury. I thought back to the seething chaos, the bouts of brutality, and all those headcases on psychoactives breaking out on fierce drifts.

I thought about how, back then I never really knew how important that time was, those encounters, how I never really cherished them until they became embalmed in my memory like so many coloured gems scuttling across the pavement.

And now it stands, The Falcon, an empty shell waiting to be filled with vacuous executives.

There were moments, caught between sequences, the paused video, the double exposed photograph, when a fragment of truth could be glimpsed, a hidden meaning exposed. It was there in those threshold spaces where the codes of the city formed constellations above the din of the street. In the bomb craters, construction sites and abandoned terraces, voices became channelled, forgotten histories exposed and trampled desires flared up in an uncanny rupturing.

This was one of the enchanted places that slipped out of sight, only to emerge and reconfigure elsewhere.

In the alleyway, another undoing encounter, climbing the fence. You sure? Yeah, the greying nets, a slight flutter, the grime and mess. A room with falling wallpaper, faded roses, mildew and moss, he cut his arm getting through the window. You sure? There were numerous portals, fluctuating and reversible like a Baroque ceiling, lenses opening onto other realms. I didn't even know him, but that's how it worked, a last grasp, a last attempt to go back. Then there would be a pause, but I had never known a full stop. In my life, there was always an adjunct, a sequel, a little bit more.

It's become an old punk cliché: 'I saw [whoever] performing at the [wherever], and I thought, if they can do that then so can I . . .' I wanted to write a story about that, from the point of view of someone who actually didn't do anything . . . And 'Fodderstompf', that great PiL dirge, which was only ever recorded (so the story goes) to fill space on an album that was rapidly nearing completion, seemed to be the perfect soundtrack . . .

Fodderstompf

Peter Wild

I was no one. Or rather I wasn't anyone. I wasn't anyone when everyone was someone.

We're talking Manchester. 1977. Everyone was someone.

Me? I was mostly oblivious. There but not there. I was at Bolton Institute of Technology, the same time as Pete Shelley and Howard Devoto. Actually think I was sitting in the refectory when they read about The Sex Pistols in the *NME*. Not that I knew them to speak to or anything. I think I was aware of them, incidentally, because Pete was on the National Committee of Part-time Students and Howard did a pub rock column for the *New Manchester Review*. They had profile. People like that, everything comes easy. There is no sense of cause and effect. Nothing comes as a surprise. Of course they brought punk to Manchester. *Of course*.

My sister was working at the Commercial Hotel in Stalybridge at the time, said some bloke called Malcolm McLaren kept ringing to try and get his band a gig there. I wasn't good at maths, didn't put two and two together, didn't know two and two went together on this occasion.

A girlfriend whose name I can't remember (I want to call her Sloppy but she can't have been called

Sloppy) dragged me along to the first Buzzcocks gig. They lasted three songs before the powers that be yanked the plug. I hated every second but Sloppy . . . she was all fired up. The sex we had that night.

Later, when the Pistols played the Lesser Free Trade Hall, I was out with a nurse, a feisty baggage called Sarah Sutton. We were smoking outside Cox's when Shelley and Devoto came by, pasting shitty flyers up everywhere. They saw me and the nurse, looked us over, decided we didn't warrant any special attention, I think.

My sister was by this point playing the Ramones' first album over and over. I'd fall asleep at nights with it playing through the wall; I'd wake in the morning, it'd still be playing.

She was going out with some lad who worked in a mail order warehouse in Bolton. Years later, she said the lad was in a band called Solstice. Turns out they supported that night at the Lesser Free Trade Hall.

This is what my life has been like. Lots of echoes without the initiating shout.

So I missed the first Pistols gig but I caught the second some months after by which point I felt a bit sour. The sound was shit. I just didn't get it. Didn't see what they saw. Everyone looking around, nodding at each other, thick as thieves. What? I wanted to yell. *What?*

Slaughter and the Dogs supported. Slaughter and the Dogs I *understood*.

They sounded like Slade next to the Pistols, course. But even so.

You don't need me to tell you who was there. All the Manchester faces. All these people who would go on to form all the bands you know and love.

But not me. I didn't do anything. Not that I was a hermit or anything. Don't get me wrong.

I remember standing at the bar at the Electric Circus once and having Ian Curtis bum a fag off me. There's a photo I think Linder Sterling took that same night: Ian and John the Postman. You can see my shoulder at the back and on the left.

Funny that, being immortalised alongside John the Postman seeing as that's what I became.

A different girl, some girl who had a name and changed it, made something up, called herself Hatchet or Ratchet or Old Tom Cratchett or something, looked like Gaye Advert if you can believe that; she dragged me to another gig by the Buzzcocks at this place called The Ranch, doesn't exist anymore, and again they only managed three songs before the management cut the power.

These boys'll go far, I remember sneering to Hatchet or Ratchet or whatever the-fuck it was she was called.

I liked the pills more than the music. Was the pills more than anything that made me a punk. I was a punk by accident. I went along to everything and hated everything and was told time and again how fucking punk that was. Got so I thought everyone hated the music. It felt like a revelation. *We all hate it*.

There was a lot of hate to go around . . .

Ah. Listen to me

Going on like some old cunt. So I've got stories. So I stood next to people who turned out to be people. So I was there. *I was there, man*. But I wasn't there. I didn't feel it like those kids felt it. I didn't get it.

You catch bits of film on TV now. How quaint it all looks.

I have a kid now. Not that he's a kid. My boy is

22. His name is Keith. I kid myself that he was named after Keith Levene but it was his mother did the honours as far as naming went. It's funny, thinking back. All of this. Being a punk. Being married. Being a dad. Being divorced. Being alone.

I'm 57. My sister is dead now. Breast cancer. Time marches on.

He asks about it all, my boy. Thinks his old dad must've been pretty cool. But I wasn't cool. This is what I tell him: I was never cool. I was just there is all, propping up the bar, scowling.

But what a time, he says. *How fucking real everything was*. This is what he says. *How fucking real*.

For him, punk was the last great hurrah, the last time anyone made any music that wasn't churned out by the man or something.

Ah, I say to him, it was all bullshit. How real it was. That's just the latest package.

I tell him, it wasn't real. It was just history happening.

I tell him: I don't think I've felt a real thing in the whole of my bloody life.

He laughs, my boy. *Keith*. He laughs and he says, How punk is *that*?

I actually think punk is overrated — it was mainly used as a platform for ambitious people and as such wasn't really that different from any other movement — but it did give some brilliant, unusual women a chance that they wouldn't have otherwise had in the boys' club that is the music industry. Poly Styrene is a case in point. A teenage hippy that later became a devotee of Krishna Consciousness, she is funny, intelligent and original. 'Germ Free Adolescents' by X-Ray Spex is an empathetic ode to eccentricity that gives hope to teenagers feeling that they are in some way different — which, let's face it, is most of them.

Germ Free Adolescents

Will Hodgkinson

'Who are these people?'

'Where is this house?'

'What is this fucking *dog*?'

Sam gave Buster a lacklustre kick. Buster released a little whimper and shuffled out of the bedroom.

'SamUEL!' went the shriek from the kitchen downstairs. 'Your dinner is already on the table and getting cold. Don't make me scream at you until my voice is hoarse. Come down here at once.'

'I honestly believe,' said Sam as he stared bleakly at his ever-narrowing yet upwards-sprouting body in the long mirror that hung on his bedroom door, 'that a mistake was made at the hospital.'

Downstairs, Sam's brother Tim was leaning back on a chair by the table, ruminating on a chunk of bread as he absently scraped the dirt underneath his fingernails with a fork. Dinner was not yet served. Their mother went backwards and forwards from kitchen to living room, slamming plates and dishes down on the round wooden table. Their father, who was wearing white Indian-style pyjamas, was sitting cross-legged on his chair, chanting the words 'om shanti'. He was staring in the middle distance with an expression that could be described as beatific or simpering depending on your levels of sympathy for this sort of thing.

'What was that shit I heard coming out of your room?' said Tim, who had dug out the dirt from the index, middle and ring fingers on his left hand and was now struggling to get the fork's prong under the nail of his thumb.

'That was "Mr Blue Sky" by ELO,' replied Sam, sitting upright at the table with his palms on the table. 'It is one of the greatest songs ever written. And you're disgusting.'

'Om shanti,' said their father.

'Have you all washed your hands?' said their mother as a casserole dish landed onto the centre of the table with an ominous thud.

'I scrubbed them for ten minutes and thirty-eight seconds before coming down,' said Sam, holding up his pale fingers, which were flecked with red patches.

Tim casually raised his head towards Sam, who was sitting opposite him. He took a small piece of bread out of his mouth, rolled it up into a ball, placed it on the back of his outstretched hand, and flicked it straight into his brother's face. Sam screamed. Tim sniggered.

'What are they doing now?' screeched their mother from the kitchen.

'Right, Timothy, that's totally outrageous behaviour,' said their father, trying to look stern. 'Just for that I'm going to fine you a pound.'

Tim slouched further back into his chair, dug into the pocket of his jeans, pulled out a pound coin, and chucked it at his father, who made a hopeless clutch in the air for it. The coin rolled off along the living room floor and came to rest under a radiator.

'It would be nice,' said their mother, as she sat down, pushed the hair away from her face and dished out the bean casserole, 'if we could at least pretend to have a normal family dinner before your father goes off to India and leaves me alone to cope with you by myself for the next four months.'

'On that note,' said their father, returning to the table after getting down on his knees to retrieve the coin, 'let's take a moment to appreciate this manna entering into our earthly bodies. Just as our souls need feeding through contemplation on their blissful eternal nature, so do the vessels containing them.'

'What, with bean casserole again?' said Tim.

'I can't eat it,' said Sam, clutching his face. 'Honestly, I'm too upset.'

'Now boys,' said their father in a light voice, 'your mother has worked hard to provide us with this nourishment . . .'

'Oh, shut up,' said their mother. 'I've got to the point where I couldn't care less if they eat it or not. They can starve for all I care.'

'It's quite nice, actually,' said Tim.

Sam managed to eat a little bit by washing every mouthful down with a glug of water. His father said that when he got back from India he would like to give a talk at the boys' school about the importance of soul consciousness.

'If you do,' said Sam, 'I'm leaving this family forever. I'm serious. I can't take it anymore. I can't take the humiliation.'

'Perhaps you could go to Switzerland,' said Tim through a mouthful of bean casserole. 'I hear it's very clean.'

Tim was going out that evening. Before he left, their mother told him to be quiet for once when he came back in, as she was sick of being woken up by him stomping about. 'It's not my fault you're such a light sleeper,' he snapped, stinking of Boots Firm Hold hairspray, as he lurched out of the front door and into the night-time world of a rock concert somewhere in Hammersmith. A few minutes later Sam went into the forbidden zone – his brother's room.

It was extremely dirty. There was an overflowing pub ashtray. A flashing beacon that had been stolen from a roadworks site had clearly not been cleaned since the theft. Apple cores rotted on piles of unwashed clothes. Sam tried not to touch anything beyond his target object: the record collection. Using the tips of his fingers he rifled through the untidy pile of records, many of them not in their sleeves. He played one called *Psychedelic Jungle* by The Cramps. He picked up an album by The Stooges. The four men in the photograph looked unhygienic. He played *Low* by David Bowie. On the front cover of the album was a picture of David Bowie with a similar hairstyle to those of the boys Sam had to run away from in the local park.

Then he pulled out a record called *Germ Free Adolescents* by X-Ray Spex. The cover featured two women and three men, all wearing brightly coloured T-shirts and dresses. They were trapped inside test tubes.

Sam put the record on the turntable. He positioned the two speakers on either side of his head, lay down on the carpet, and let the songs play out. All the things he disliked about a lot of his brother's records – poor sound quality, out of tune vocals – were here, but somehow they were appealing. The lead singer couldn't really sing, but Sam found that her voice affected him in a way that took him by surprise, like her essence was laid bare. Then came the song called 'Germ Free Adolescents'.

Sam sat completely still. If the singer – whose

name he had just discovered from the liner notes was Poly Styrene — had been singing in Swahili, the melody in her voice would have still stopped him in his tracks, but as she sang about cleanliness being her obsession, about brushing her teeth three times a day, about the virtues of a nice-smelling deodorant, he started to cry.

'Jesus Christ,' he said, softly, as the song came to an end. 'She's singing about me.'

The next day at school, Sam was late for double maths after spending quarter of an hour in the toilets, scrubbing his hands. He refused to play football in the afternoon on account of the fact that the pitch was covered in germs. He ended up sitting in detention, which was preferable anyway. The day after that he succeeded in stealing a bright-yellow T-shirt of his brother's from the clean washing pile outside the downstairs toilet.

By the time his father had left for India in search of soul consciousness, Sam was scrubbing the bathroom with disinfectant every evening after his brother and his mother had used it, in preparation for his own time in there, which was between 11pm and 1am. Sometimes he sat in the bath for up to an hour, wondering why the world outside this tiled sanctuary seemed to get dirtier by the day.

Buster was banned from Sam's bedroom. His mother wasn't, but she rarely had reason to go in there any more since it was always so tidy and clean, and Sam was insisting on doing his own laundry, separate from the rest of the family's clothes. Tim was increasingly absent. Sam was devastated to discover that X-Ray Spex had split up about five years previously, but intrigued to hear that their day-glow-clad lead singer Poly Styrene had devoted herself to Krishna Consciousness, which wasn't so different from the path his father had taken.

'I think I'm in love,' he said to himself one evening, as *Germ Free Adolescents* went round and round on the record player and Sam gazed blankly at the test tube album cover, willing himself into a trance.

Cathy Curtis had slipped a couple of messages to him, once during geography and once during English. She seemed to want to come round to his house. He told her that it was a bit difficult now that his mother was going through such a hard time, what with his father being in Hollywood making blockbuster science fiction movies and so on, but one afternoon she turned up anyway and his mother let her in.

'Shit!' whispered Sam from his bedroom window, looking down as Cathy rang the doorbell and stood in the rain in her duffel coat and bunches.

'He's in his room,' said his mother as more than the usual amount of footsteps padded up the stairs. 'If you can manage to get him further than the bathroom you'll have achieved more than me.'

There was a knock on the door, followed by his mother's head poking into the room. She looked strangely hopeful. 'There's somebody here to see you,' she said in a wide-eyed whisper.

'Tell her I'm not in!' said Sam. 'Tell her I'm ill!' He jumped into his bed and pulled the duvet up over his head.

'Don't be ridiculous,' said his mother hotly. 'Come in, Cathy. He's over there.'

'Hi Sam,' said Cathy, standing in the doorway and raising a palm upwards. 'How are you?'

Sam stuck his head up over the duvet. 'Argh! What are you doing?'

'What do you mean?'

'You're wearing shoes. There are probably a million different sub-stratas of dirt on the bottom of them. Please take them off.'

'Oh,' said Cathy, looking down at the Converse basketball boots that she had only bought two days previously, after months of saving up for them. This was the first time she had worn them out of the house and she was shocked at her own oversight: she never wore shoes indoors at her own home. 'I'm sorry.'

'I don't mean to be rude,' said Sam. 'It's just that I'm trying to maintain a reasonable standard of cleanliness. Would you like a cup of tea?'

'No thanks. May I sit down?'

'Over there.'

He pointed to a small wooden chair in the corner of the room.

They sat in silence for a while until Sam said: 'Would you like to hear my new record?'

'Oh, yes please. But can I come and sit next to you on the bed? This chair is really uncomfortable.'

Sam frowned, and then said, 'Hold on a minute.'

He opened a cupboard and took out from the top shelf a neatly folded blanket, which he laid out on the end of the bed. 'Sit on that,' he said.

He put on 'Germ Free Adolescents'. Cathy wasn't allowed to talk during its duration. They sat next to each other on the bed. 'Sam,' she said quietly, looking at him, but he raised a finger to his lips and pointed at the record player. She moved up closer. He moved an inch or two away, thinking she wouldn't notice.

'What do you think of that, then?' said Sam.

'I love it,' she said solemnly. 'It's the best song I've ever heard.'

Sam nodded.

'Can I have a look through your record collection?'

'Yes you can, but wait a minute,' he said. He went over to a desk by the window, opened the drawer, and pulled out a pair of clear polythene surgical gloves.

'Here,' he said, holding the dangling gloves up at chest height before him, arms outstretched. 'I must insist you put these on first.'

After listening to the whole of the X-Ray Spex album as well as *Out of the Blue* by ELO, Cathy and Sam compared deodorant brands. 'You can't use any that smell of anything,' said Cathy. 'They're all disgusting. You need to use an antiperspirant that is odourless. I recommend Mum.'

'Wow.'

'You use mouthwash as well as toothpaste, obviously,' said Cathy, 'but do you floss?'

'I don't like it,' said Sam, rubbing his teeth. 'It makes my gums bleed.'

'Why do you think that is? It's because your gums are unhealthy and infected. If you flossed regularly that wouldn't happen. What do you want, cavities? Actually, all this talk of bathrooms is making me need to go to one. Where is it?'

'Hang on a minute.' Sam took out a piece of paper and a pen and drew a map to the nearest public convenience. 'There you go. Should only take you five or ten minutes there and back.'

'I don't use public conveniences,' she replied, crunching up the map into a little ball and throwing it across the room, where it landed in the bin.

'No. No, of course not. Who does? The bathroom's down the end of the corridor.'

His mother appeared at the door. 'Is everything alright? Can I get you two anything?'

'Leave us alone!' he hissed, but for the first time in a long time his mother detected a smile lightening his taut face. Then he said in a conspiratorial whisper, pointing to the corridor: 'She's in the bathroom.'

Sam's mother raised a thumb and said, 'If she wants to stay the night, that's fine by me.' Sam shooed her away.

Then the bathroom door opened and Sam's mother darted downstairs. Sam frantically straightened the duvet. Cathy came back in. She had taken her bunches out, and for the first time she didn't look like the slightly annoying classmate Sam had known for the last five years but had never really paid any attention to. She looked clean. She sat down next to him on the bed, and not on her designated blanket.

'Have you ever wondered,' she said, 'how many germs go from one mouth to another when two people kiss?'

Sam gulped. 'I . . . I . . . I . . . think about germs quite a lot . . .'

'But my mouth is cleaner than yours because I've just cleaned my teeth. So if I kiss you, I'll actually be wiping out some of your germs with the power of my disinfected mouth.'

Cathy got up and put the stylus of the record player down onto 'Germ Free Adolescents'. She didn't don the surgical gloves to do so. Then she sat back on the bed next to Sam. Then Cathy and Sam kissed each other for the first time.

The following morning they shared the same toothbrush.

'Get Yourself Killed' by The Tickets. . . . Back when I was a teenager I listened to wall-to-wall punk obscurities (alternating these with soul, funk and all sorts of other music) and this tune had a particularly memorable chorus that has just stuck in my head for the past thirty years.

Get Yourself Killed

Stewart Home

I'd got on the train at Waterloo and was sitting with my nose stuck in Mickey Spillane's pulp monstrosity *One Lonely Night*. I was on my way to visit a friend in Surbiton. It was the early 80s and back then you had a choice of smoking and non-smoking carriages. I chose the latter because I disliked passive smoking, which was unavoidable in many of the places I frequented at the time. I chose the empty end of a carriage, but before the train moved off two squaddies and their wives got on and sat close to me. The men were non-commissioned officers, corporals. They were older than me, in their late-20s or early-30s, and looked ridiculous in their neatly pressed uniforms.

'I want to smoke. I'm going to another carriage,' one of the women announced.

'Just smoke here, let's not move,' her husband replied.

'If you light up here I'm gonna pull the fag outta your mouth,' I told the woman as she got a pack of B&H from her bag.

'If you do that I'll beat the crap out of you!' her husband shouted.

'I wouldn't if I was you,' I shot back, 'you'll get in a shit load of trouble being under military as well as civil law. You've got a lot more to worry about on that score than me. It's great on civvy street!'

The man's wife put her fags back in her bag and was shooting her husband looks, and holding onto him to discourage him from getting up and starting anything. I was smirking and the corporal caught the smile on my face.

'What's wrong with you? Can't you respect a uniform?'

'Join the army and get yourself killed!' I laughed, putting some lyrics by a defunct East London punk band called The Tickets to good use.

'Are you one of those peace protesters then?' The corporal demanded.

'Me, a peace protester? No mate, no. You've got me all wrong. Do you know what I am?'

'No,' the squaddie was flummoxed.

'I'll tell you what I am, I'm a student and I study philosophy. That means your taxes pay for me to sit on my arse and do nothing all day. And I'll tell you something else, when I come out of college I'm gonna sit behind a desk being paid four times as much as you and not having to die for my country. I'll be ordering people like you into wars, not dying in them.'

'It's people like you that have ruined this country,' the corporal's wife snapped at me.

'I ain't finished ruining it yet.'

The squaddies and their wives sat in a gloomy silence. I'd pulled off an A1 wind-up. I despised the British army and the patriotic bollocks that went along with it, and I knew coming out with a peace and love line was never effective on squaddies. I didn't want to sit in an office for most of my life and be rewarded at the age of 65 with a gold watch. But that was something the squaddies could relate to. I'd used the line about desk jobs to demoralise them. Believe it or not I was a philosophy student at the time, but only because being on a full maintenance grant meant getting more money than signing on the dole. I had no intention of getting a job like my mates from school, who'd left at sixteen for factory jobs and the army. Disco and northern soul were the big musical cultures at my school. I'd liked a lot of soul and funk, still do, but I'd been the first kid on the block to get into punk rock, and as a result back then I was still looking forward to a lifetime of progressive unemployment.

Poly Styrene's voice holds the essence of punk for me. It's a raucous, abandoned, chaotic and real call to arms. I think X-Ray Spex are the perfect punk band, one classic album of two-minute aural assaults and an inspirational, hyper-intelligent female front person who was unafraid to be herself and never sold out. My first boyfriend put this song on a tape for me when I was fifteen and I suppose that's why I have always associated it with being young, carefree and in love.

The Day the World Turned Day-Glo

Kate Jackson

THE DAY THE WORLD TURNED DAY-GLO
UK chart position 23, April 1978.

20 April 1998

Maria, eighteen. Daydreamer. Shop assistant. Aspiring poet.

Today I like Frank O'Hara and filter coffee and Campari and bitter lemon. In a vague attempt to feel sophisticated I am listening to Anita O'Day. I hope she will conjure some sort of inspiration but all she is doing is reminding me of hours spent on the shop floor in Accessorize, where jazz divas blend into The Corrs and Gabrielle in an effortless lifestyle choice. Who makes those Accessorize tapes anyway? They come sealed in a special delivery bag every month, wrapped with extra strong gaffer tape to prevent tampering. Some middle manager bored shitless in a meeting at the head office in London, looking out the window at the Westway, thinking about what time they will get out and how busy M&S will be.

'The Corrs?'

'Fine.'

'Anita O'Day?'

'Does she make you want to go out and buy a pair of velour gloves after a manicure? Well fine.'

Never mind that we might permanently ruin a shop assistant's love of her records forever.

Outside it's raining a torrent over the B&Q warehouse. Yes, I'm still not where I want to be. I haven't found out where that is yet, so I'll stay in my room and wait for the need for it to pass. I still don't understand time. How things can be so very different now and yet still feel so very wrong. On a day off I would normally go into town and have a look in a few charity shops, look at the books for inspiration and try and find 7" singles for less than 50p, which is pretty hard these days. Charity is suddenly wise to the value of records. Charity knows what's cool and what's not. Gone are the days of finding someone's discarded punk collection at ten pence a piece. I can't be bothered with charity shopping today.

Frank O'Hara didn't seem to like titles very much. Well, his most catchy poem is called 'Poem', not 'Lana Turner Has Collapsed!' but everyone just calls it that anyway. And why not? He's dead so people can call his poems what they like.

Five to two. If I was at work I'd just be going on lunch. Last lunch hour, makes the afternoon shorter. I should be doing something useful rather than just sitting here waiting for my life to start. I'm finding it hard to motivate myself now that you've broken my heart. You made me feel so inadequate. You told me I was your soul mate, that you and I were magic, that the day you met me was the day the world turned day-glo. I still can't believe that you could say that shit. How could you invent those feelings? I would have loved you forever. You bastard.

'The Day the World Turned Day-Glo' is a great song. If I listen to it will you come back to me?

20 April 1998

Chrissie, 35. Retail buyer. Mother of one. Unfulfilled romantic.

'Good morning ladies and gentlemen, this is your captain speaking. As you may have gathered we have started our descent into London's Heathrow. There's a bit of traffic but we should be on schedule to land in about twenty-five minutes' time. Weather in London is currently cloudy with a slight southwesterly breeze and it's mild for the time of year with a ground temperature of fourteen degrees. I hope you've had a pleasant flight with British Airways and look forward to taking you up again in the near future'

'Is there a future in this? I'm thirty-five years old and I don't think I love you. I think we should spend sometime apart.' How has it only taken a fucking flight time for me to notice? I'd never be able to say that to him though, not really. Not ever. I wonder if he'll even notice that I'm not the same. I can put on a good act; I must've been doing it for fucking years. How did I not notice? Get through customs, go to the toilet, fix my face, pick up my baggage, and walk through arrivals and smile. That's all I have to do.

'Excuse me, madam, is your seatbelt fastened?'

'Sorry?'

'Your seatbelt? The captain has switched on the fasten seatbelt signs now.'

'Oh, sorry, I was miles away.'

If I hadn't seen James this week would I have felt like this? Is it so wrong to feel like this? We only chatted for a second and I mean, he's married and I'm married. It was a long, long time ago. He's looking older anyway, no question. He's not what he was, but neither am I. That feeling though. The chemical reaction that spreads across the brain like a gin rush and the tingling in my hands, in my feet and, oh God, in my groin. That feeling came back. There we were standing on the same street, in the same city for the first time in ten years and it was still there. Now I can't fucking forget it.

'Ladies and gentlemen, the seatbelt sign is still on so please remain seated until the aircraft has come to a complete stop and the seatbelt sign has been switched off.'

Jesus, I didn't even notice us land. Heathrow, how many times have I been here? Why is this time any different? Usually a business trip is just soulless Marriott hotel rooms and a guilt-free late-night drink. I'm always missing David and Lucy, calling all the time to see that he picked her up from nursery or ballet, romancing the English fields as the plane circles over the countryside, looking out for our house but never really knowing where it is. Today I feel nothing. I'm not even anxious. Jesus.

'Thank you madam. Thank you sir, thank you madam.' Silence. 'Thank you madam.'

They never thank me, always everyone else. Perhaps those people look more like proper human beings. Perhaps I am not worth thanking. I am not someone who complains so I am not important enough to thank, perhaps I am still a teenager to them. There'll be a much more noteworthy adult, someone with more money, more class, more cash, in front of me and behind me so I get lost between earnest thank yous.

Passport control. UK Border. No man's land. I am in no man's land. If I leave him, she'll suffer; if I stay, I'll suffer. Perhaps these are the sacrifices that adults have to make. Perhaps I've been making this sacrifice for years already. Why did I have to wake up? It wasn't just seeing James; I was ready to flee before I left. I didn't want to call home all week; the only reason I did was to hear Lucy's voice, I didn't want to listen to him going on about the washing machine and the car.

'Step forward, madam.'

I'll go to the ladies now, fix my face before I get my bags.

God, I am not a teenager. I am not even young anymore. My hair is wrecked and my face is puffy. What did I think? Did I think I was glamorous this week? Trotting down 32nd Street thinking I was Jackie Kennedy. It was all an illusion.

'Hhhhammm, I have everything I wanted when I was a little girl and I'm still not satisfied. How can I be a good mother and wife then, how?'

Time slows down sometimes. One step follows another, follows another. The mind goes blank and all sound feels distant, as if trying to listen to a coastal party from a submarine. Arrivals. Nothing to Declare. I have nothing to declare.

'Hello, darling!'

'Mummy! Look. Mummy, look! Daddy bought me crayons!'

'Wow, sweetheart, they're beautiful. Show me? Have you done a drawing for Mummy?'

He looks more handsome than I remember. He's let himself go 'cos I've been away, stubble, scruffy jacket, uncombed hair. How could I ever have contemplated leaving him, taking her away from him? It's all gone now, it was all an illusion.

'I've got a taxi waiting, c'mon Chrissie. It's good to see you, baby.'

'How's Lucy been?'

'Just fine, we've been just fine. We missed you though! Did you bring us any presents back?'

I haven't. Oh God, I haven't.

'Yes, darling, wait till we get home. Lucy! Come here. What are you doing?'

'Counting cars.'

'What's this then? Been on holiday have we? Little girl's first trip abroad? Where to, mate?'

'Daddy said you could make up words from car number plates. KAP! LAX! DOG!'

'Dog is a real word darling'

God, this car stinks.

'Twenty years ago today this band performed on *Top of the Pops*. You wouldn't see anything like this on the show now, this is Poly Styrene and her X-Ray Spex, "The Day the World Turned Day Glo".'

Shit. James. X-Ray Spex were one of his favourite bands. I'll never see him again. Just block him out. I have my family right here in this car. Don't cry Chrissie, don't cry.

20 April 1998

Richard, 42. Taxi driver. Broken family man.
Perennially single.

'I clambered over mounds and mounds of polystyrene
foam and fell into a swimming pool filled with fairy
snow. And watched the world turn day-glo you know,
you know. The world turned day-glo you know.'

'What's this then? Been on holiday have we? Little
girl's first trip abroad?'

Talk to yourself, Richard. Ah, X-Ray Spex, April
1978, let's see . . . March '77 was The Clash at the Corn
Exchange so must've seen X-Ray Spex about a month
after that at the Roxy in London. Ah, The Roxy, closed
down around the time this single was released. Shame.

'Where to, mate?'

No, that can't be right, or can it? Yes. That makes
sense, never went to The Roxy with Wendy so must've
been around April '78 'cos I met her around then.

'DOG'

'Dog is a real word, darling!'

Dogs, love 'em, mutts-ah. Wendy was never keen
so we never had one. Wouldn't have helped anyway, she
didn't want those things. Kids, dogs, dirty laundry, she
just took speed and cried all the time, even after we were
married. Sat there speeding her tits off, I did too, even
if we had nowhere to go but up to bed. There was a time
when bed wasn't the torture chamber it is today. Bah.

'Mummy, why are you crying?'

'I'm not, darling'

'Yes you are, Mummy, your face is wet.'

Your face is wet, yes she is crying, he's ignoring it,
kid's confused. Families, who'd have 'em? If I get these

dropped by four I can be parked up by five and in the boozer by ten past. Several Kronenbergs. Maybe I should call Wendy, get in touch, see how she is these days. Perhaps she'd like to go to a gig or something, or just have a beer sometime. Why not? Nothing to lose, Richard. If you don't go knocking she'll never answer. Nah, she's bound to be shacked up with some tossah, or married again with a horde of kids and a bloody dog.

'Humph.'

'Sorry?'

'Eh? Oh nothing, 'scuse me.'

Blimey, it was only a sigh. Yeah I remember that X-Ray Spex gig, heh, marvelous, she was marvelous Poly Styrene, not half, yes please, sir.

Wish I could've seen them with Wendy. Went to so many gigs together in '78 and '79. The Clash, the Buzzcocks, The Fall – ah. Joe Strummer gave her a set list one night and I knew then the girl was special. Married her in the summer of '79 but she soon got bored. Moved out after six months. Said she'd met someone else, that I was depressing, boring, an old fart. All 'cos I wanted a family. I know we were only in our early 20s but she was the girl for me. She was just a kid really. What did I expect? It wasn't her fault.

20 April 1998

Wendy, 40. Social worker. Permanently exhausted. Trying to make everyone happy.

'Maria! Maria! What you doing up there? It's gone one, don't you think it's time you were up?'

That girl's been so difficult lately. I just can't seem to get through to her. Even when I do get to talk to her it's like she's not really there. She certainly doesn't listen to me. It's like something's broken in her. She never used to be like this; we've always been so close, like sisters. I just don't understand it. If it's a boy she's having trouble with, she knows she can talk to me.

'Maria! Come on, I'll make you some lunch'

She's been skiving off work and lying to me about it. I know she has. Her boss rang yesterday to ask where she was and I lied for her, said she was ill. I'm too soft on her I know, but I used to do the same when I was her age. Today's her day off anyway she says, but what if she's lying about that too? Am I a mug? I just want to help her and if she's not happy I want to know about it, but she won't tell me anything. I'm so busy at work too that maybe I haven't noticed her becoming unhappy. Maybe she's got an eating disorder or something like that and she doesn't want to tell me. Christ, I'm a social worker, I should notice if my own daughter is ill. She's usually so outgoing. Oh, Christ.

'Maria, sweetheart, come down!'

Maybe I shouldn't have asked her to pay me rent. I wanted to teach her about the real world like other parents do. I have friends who use that approach and their kids are fine with it, they can't wait to leave home and travel the bloody world. Not Maria. She's so independent in some ways but in others, I don't know. Maybe it's because I've always spoilt her. I don't think she understands that when she leaves this house she'll have to pay council tax, rent and bills all on her own. All she spends her money on is records and booze. Mind you, so did I when I was eighteen. I remember my David Bowie obsession, before I moved to London, before I met Richard.

Ah, Richard. Bless him. Wasn't cut out for life in the real world either.

'Oh hello, darling, are you OK? Have you been in bed all morning? Do you want something to eat?

'No, Mum, I'm fine. I just came down to say hello.'

'Well that's nice but you have to eat. You'll waste away.'

'No really, mum, I'm fine. I'm just not hungry'

'Maria, I need to talk to you. I'm worried. You're not eating and you're lying to me about work. Has something happened? Are you in trouble? Are you not feeling well?'

'I'm fine'

'Come on, darling, tell me. Please'

'It's nothing, I'm just not like everyone else that's all.'

'What do you mean?'

'Nothing.'

'Please tell me sweetheart.'

'NO.'

'OK, OK. What's that you're listening to?'

'X-Ray Spex.'

'Oh yes, it's 'The Day the World Turned Day-Glo' isn't it?'

'How do you know that?'

'Well, I used to be really into this song back in '77 and '78. So did your father.'

'What was he like, Mum? Did you love him?'

'He was kind, generous and completely useless. He drank too much; in fact he's probably dead by now if he carried on drinking that way. I don't know. Once I knew I was pregnant with you, though, I knew I had to end it. I loved him, but I already loved you more, I loved you more.'

'Do you ever think about him?'

'Sometimes, really only when I hear music from then. I hope he's well and has settled down with a woman he loves. Someone who had the strength to keep him out of the pub. I couldn't do it. I couldn't look after him and look after you. I loved you too much. Why? Do you think about him, sweetheart?'

'I have been recently. Jason dumped me and I don't believe in love anymore.'

'Oh, darling, come here. Jason wasn't worth it anyway, full of himself, not good enough for you. Give me a cuddle. You know, you can try and meet him, I mean your dad, if you want to. I'll help you find him.'

'Thanks, Mum.'

'Look, I'll show you something. It's the only thing I have left from then.'

'What is it?'

'It's a set list. Joe Strummer gave it to me in 1978, the first time we saw The Clash together at the Camden Music Machine. He proposed to me that night, your dad. I said yes even though I knew then it wasn't right. You can have it if you want.'

"I actually wrote this short piece before I had settled on my chosen song. So, I had to read the text over and realised there was only one song that really represented the idea I was trying to convey. The concept of the passage is that the original premise of punk was realised and actually changed everything. That it took hold of the country and overthrew the pontificating bureaucrats, the blind, ignorant conservatives and the passive aggressive bourgeoisie and tipped the nation into pure anarchy. So choosing the Pistols' 'Anarchy in the UK' is self-explanatory. Though I cant say I like the Pistols' music too much, I respect anyone who has screamed and shouted against these sham ideologies that we are fed from a young age, the people who have stood up and plainly said, 'NO, I wIll not have my mind fiddled with.'"

Anarchy in the UK

Edward Larrikin

things had changed. by the time the sun was up and it was light again, the punk song had tipped the satellite nation on its head, it had become the mantra echoing thru the palace gates and slithering out into the ventricles of the city. the citizens communicated solely in screams – abbreviations of abbreviations – and wild gesticulations. all pretensions melted down into a base form of nothingness. there were no decisions made, no major schools of thought, no high horses to be ridden. the queen was a gambler; she slapped her cats arse sucklers around 40 sovereign a day. guzzled electric white ace and shaved a zig zag thru her blue rinse. her nipple tassels were the colour of the pavements and her black suspenders tucked in a flick knife with the engraving – bondage Lizz. 'if you can't beat 'em join 'em,' she spat. DEAD STATE. the radio was a punk and that put a stop to that silent city perforated with razor sharp wails of former politicians who had ridded of their mohicans and become self-imposed alopecia kid soldiers. except for these shit-sucking sheep all old people were dead.

a spray of fizzling violence leapt off the face of the suffuse stream. the long piddle thru the city was now two banks of sludge where the younger ranks built silt warehouses and pissed them away again. by the time the sun had hit its peak, automobiles and trams became the drum kits of punk city. they lay on their sides on what used to be parliament square but now was a wasteland of churchill rubble. young men salivating in a paradise of violent freedom banged the fresh bones of chief inspectors, sheriffs, priests, landlords, and council members into these quickly forgotten obsolete transports. the sound of ancient soul rebels who abandoned their tribes in an autonomous fug rang out from the bashing shrill of the metal, the shattering of the glass, the howling annihilation of the engines. the females stood pissing on the gentlemen's clubs, on the empty bodies of conservative bureaucrats, they shat pus into the rugby pub and left their fathers to drown in swimming pools of hot leather and st georges stitch. they swung from rooftop to memorial, from factory to hotel, demolishing the ordinary, melting the extraordinary to nothing, no past, no future.

the song had infected the air. its pervasive, rumbling sweep had knocked the peoples into some kind of feral rampage. they lived for nothing but destruction and reaction. the punk hymn reverberating around their bodies as they set to work this wasn't nihilism – this was focused, abject revolt they had so many reasons to spit and shit and kick out and they did.

they opened up the sewers and sailed the bill of rights out thru a sea of waste, they flushed the government house down a public toilet. they doused wood lane in a fluent acidic spume, taking with it fleet street, liverpool street, harley street and the chelsea barracks. They chopped and snorted the insipid brick dust that fell from the ceilings of the chamber of commerce that danced thru the air in the civic centre that clogged the air vents of the museums, job centres and health clubs.

as the sun fell out of reach and slumped behind the empty buildings and office blocks, the sky came alight with splinters of flame and vertical tunnels of thick industrial smoke rising from the many street bonfires that put an end to media, to printed word, to the dying purple cunt of celebrity, to the dribbling broadcaster and commentator. commentator hear this, your days are over and nobody wants you.

the city was decimated. all that remained were our punk heroes gobbing in the icy rains that chilled the day's madness. as the sun began to rise again, he dropped a burning spear of phlegm on the exhausted face of the earth and it all started again.

This Iggy Pop single was released at the end of the 70s and the end of the punk scene of which Iggy was designated 'godfather'. Here the ageing rock'n'roller appears to be taking a rueful look at himself. The music is suitably shambolic, raucously referencing Elvis Presley's '(Marie's the Name of) His Latest Flame' before dissolving into some desultory Sex Pistols-style riffing. The sentiments and mood of this song combined with the musings of the late Johnny Thunders on the album *Bootlegging the Bootleggers* were the inspiration for the character of Mickey in this story.

Loco Mosquito

Jay Clifton

Cashel O'Keefe decided that he had a lot going for him: he was 24, raffishly handsome, a great raconteur and a fine *scordato* saxophone player. He was also drunk as hell, and having trouble walking in a straight line.

Cashel himself, an aficionado of metaphor, would have told you that last observation could be used to explain his whole problem in relation to life.

That may be so, but the present reality was that Cashel's legs were going improvisational on him. As he staggered along Springfield Road towards his current temporary residence (at least he hoped it were temporary), he had as much control over their direction as his fellow band members had over him when he broke into a *scordato* sax solo on stage. Some cynics described his solos as tuneless, but they were surely the kind of people who had never even *encountered* the word *scordato*, let alone appreciated it as a musical approach.

It would be difficult to gauge just how much Cashel had had to drink at the venue. Backstage was the band's rider, a generous amount of chilled lager he could drink for free, but he'd been seen at the bar too, throwing back whisky shots. Probably he'd been drinking steadily since midday. It was Saturday, after all.

But if any of Cashel's friends stopped to think about it, they rarely saw him sober anymore on *any* day of the week, and when they did, he appeared hung-over and pervasively despondent. He was still friendly and occasionally droll in this condition, but his head would hang low, he seemed physically listless and he had the look of someone waiting for life to start again with the next drink, or the next line of cocaine. The coke was something he'd come to enjoy more and more in the last year thanks to the generosity of the band's high-flying lead singer, a mysterious by-way-of-London heartthrob whose lush lifestyle seemed unhampered by the usual limitations of the kind of income received from a seven-hour working week in an antiquarian Brighton bookshop. At least the CC had been free at the beginning, a 'CC Rider', so to speak. Now the band put up equal shares for it before their gigs.

Cashel's face had become in that time as pallid as a *fin-de-siècle* poet's, a likeness augmented by Cashel's pencil thin moustache and oiled-down hair. He was getting greyhound skinny, and he seemed to sweat a lot for a young man, even for summer. All in all he looked terrible – or great, depending on how far you bought into the phrase, 'Live fast, die young, leave a good-looking corpse.'

Not that Cashel was looking for help. He didn't need anything but to get his exhausted self home and flattened out on his bed with the falafel he had stashed in the vegetable container of the refrigerator where none of his motley housemates would find it, or so he hoped. He hadn't eaten anything more than a packet of salt and vinegar crisps all day, and that falafel was presently more attractive to him than

Brigitte Bardot in *Viva Maria*, or indeed his vexatious blonde bombshell of a girlfriend, Evelyn Bell.

He didn't want to think about Evelyn tonight. Didn't he think about her enough as it was? She made sure of that. When he wasn't working at the retro clothing store or at his shitty telephone research job, he was always running some errand for her – picking up some dog food for the chihuahua, which she had strangely called Maple (after maple syrup, perhaps, or 'my pal' – who knew? Who cared?), or running some trashy paperback novel and a pint of milk over to one of Evelyn's girlfriends who worked in a little clothes shop a couple of blocks from Evelyn's hair salon. As if Cashel didn't have his own things to do on a Saturday. He did these stupid favours for Evelyn, because – well, whatever the reason, he did them. And did she thank him for it? Did she hell! She acted more like it was *he* who should be thanking *her*!

And she flirted outrageously. She was a fox, and in those black-and-white gossamer outfits of hers she drew a lot of lustful male attention when she walked into a room. Cashel used to *like* that, it made him feel more like a rock star. But that was in earlier days, when Evelyn would stay close to him all night, when she would be at the front of the stage when they came on to play, scarlet nails wrapped around a JD and coke, poised like a catwalk model, batting her lashes at him, a sparkle in those Bermuda-blue eyes of hers, a picture of perfervidity.

Perfervid: he had found this unusual word in the dictionary (his favourite book) and liked its particular sense. It meant, 'Very fervid; ardent; eager'. It sat right above 'perfidious', which meant, 'Faithless; deceitful; treacherous'. The way Cashel saw it, Evelyn had moved from perfervidity to perfidy through some mysterious coup d'état of the heart.

She had always flirted a bit when they were out together, that was her way, and Cashel hadn't cared because things were good between them and she knew where to draw the line. But these days she went all out to provoke him. She'd spend all evening talking to this guy or that, leaning in close, batting those eyelashes at her selected mark and generally being obnoxious.

For the last four nights she had slept on a sofa in the backroom of her hair salon (Extensions – her clients were almost exclusively Goths of the well-heeled variety and fortunately Brighton seemed to have a lot of them) rather than go back with him to his place. He knew that's where she was tonight because he'd gone over there after the gig and knocked on the glass door. A light went on in the backroom but Evelyn didn't come out so he called her on his mobile phone and asked her to come to the door. She did, but she just stayed on her side of the glass and told him to go home. She wanted to sleep, she said.

But Cashel O'Keefe had decided that he had a lot going for him: he was 24, ruffishly handsome, a great raconteur and a fine *scordato* saxophone player. And as he made his unsteady way up the steps to his front door he drew an uplifting conclusion from that: if she wanted to keep *him*, Evelyn had better watch her step.

As if to punctuate this thought, his right knee suddenly buckled and he plunged headlong through the window of the basement flat below.

The next thing he was aware of, he was lying on a floor. It had a carpet which was something on the side of comfort for him, though not a great deal. His body hurt all over and he was afraid of moving it, at least for the moment. There was a faint buzzing in his ears. He curled his fingers a little, and was glad to find that he could feel some sensation in them. He kept his eyes shut. It was actually kind of peaceful and quiet, apart from the occasional sound of footsteps from the footpath above, and the slight crackle of glass splinters when he moved the heel of his boot. But gradually the buzzing sound in his ears became louder, until it was as loud as an electric handsaw.

He forced himself to open his eyes. What he saw couldn't possibly be right, so he shut his eyes, told himself to get a grip, counted to ten and opened his eyes again.

There was no getting around it: planted on the carpet a few inches from his left heel was a big, ugly, black mosquito, the size of an adult human being. It was looking at its own proboscis, a strangely elegant rapier-like organ, inserted in the crook of his exposed left arm. In addition to the buzzing that seemed to come from its vibrating gauzy wings, it was making a nasty, mucal gasping sound every ten or so seconds. When this *thing* noticed Cashel staring at it, it immediately detached itself from Cashel and shifted itself slightly.

'I apologise, but I got low blood sugar,' said the mosquito in what sounded to Cashel like a New York low-rent accent. The tone was companionable. 'I'm Mickey. What's your name, fella?'

'Maaaaah,' was all that Cashel could say in return.

The mosquito repeated the noise a few times – 'mah . . . mah . . . ' – like it was thinking something over. Then it said ebulliently, 'Marlon? Is that your name, fella? Marlon, what a *cool* fuckin' name!

'I gotta tell ya, I love Marlon Brando's movies. Like that one where he's running a motorcycle gang, and this Podunk waitress comes up to him and says 'Hey what

are you against?' – and he says, 'What have you got?'
What have you got! Sharp as knives. Woah . . . Excuse
me, here, low blood sugar . . .'

Mickey the mosquito reinserted his proboscis in
Cashel's arm and stayed quiet for about a minute while
he drank and breathed mucally. Cashel watched in rapt
horror.

'Fuck me,' gasped Mickey appreciatively, remov-
ing his organ with a dainty final flick. 'What? Did you
have your blood replaced with sangria?'

Cashel looked at Mickey blankly.

'That's potent stuff,' said Mickey, indicating a
small pool of Cashel's spilled blood soaking darkly into
the carpet.

'Drank quite a bit,' said Cashel slowly. He propped
himself up on one elbow and moved his left arm so that
it was less available.

'No kidding,' said Mickey. 'What did you have
tonight? I used to like a drink myself. Nowadays I find
it hard to get served in bars. You can probably guess
why. Tell me what you had.'

'Stella.'

'What's that?'

'It's a Belgian beer, pretty strong. You never had
that?'

'Never did.'

'Well, you're not missing much. It gets you where
you want to go.'

'I hear ya,' said Mickey. He appeared to be settling
himself down, and if he weren't such a creepy mutant
insect, Cashel might almost have thought he looked
wistful.

'I had quite a few whiskies too,' said Cashel,
preferring conversation to silence.

'What brand?'

'Jamesons.'

'You prefer the Irish whiskies huh? I mean to Bourbon or Scotch?'

'They had a special offer on it.'

'You know what I used to love drinking? Bushmills or Black Bush. You ever had Black Bush Irish whisky?'

'Yeah, Mickey, I have,' said Cashel after a moment. He felt he now had the measure of what was going on here and so he no longer felt intimidated by Mickey the mosquito.

'You mind if I have another drink?' the big insect asked hopefully.

'Sorry, Mickey, the bar's closed,' said Cashel, pushing aside Mickey's proboscis. 'Anyway, you aren't real. There's a good reason no one talks about their encounters with man-sized mosquitoes and that's because they don't fucking exist outside of dreams. The situation is thus: I am dreaming and you are a product of my feverish mind, which is being perfidious. But the game is up my freaky friend, it's time for you to fuck off or turn into an ice-cream sundae.'

Mickey twitched.

'So that's the way it is, huh Marlon?' he said after a pause.

'That's the way it is,' replied Cashel evenly.

'All right,' said Mickey, moving back a little and kind of straightening up.

'You're the big man here right? And I'm just a figment of your fevered mind. So you *turn* me into an ice-cream sundae. Go ahead, I fuckin' *dare* you. And if you can do it, you can fuckin' *eat* me!'

For the next seven minutes they watched each

other balefully while Cashel tried to apply his mind to Mickey's transformation.

Mickey finally broke the stalemate.

'Did it work?' he asked, with poorly veiled sarcasm. 'What fuckin' flavour am I?'

'All right, Mickey, what's going on?'

'Oh,' said the insect with a hollow laugh. 'So now you want to know what's going on. Hah! Well, I'd like to know too. I didn't choose to be here. Where *are* we anyway? What town?'

Cashel told him.

'Where's that? What country?'

'You're kidding,' groaned Mickey when Cashel told him, 'Tell me you're kidding.'

When Cashel shook his head, the mosquito slumped to the floor.

'I get moved around more than a Haitian family on welfare.'

'What's wrong with England?'

'Nothing I guess, if you're a mammal.' Mickey looked at Cashel pitiably. 'It's too cold here for the likes of me,' he explained. 'I could fuckin' die.'

'It's summer, Mickey,' said Cashel. He was almost starting to feel sympathy for his strange companion.

'I wasn't always a big fuckin' mosquito,' said Mickey. 'I used to be a man. I was a musician. A pretty good one at that.'

'I'm a musician too,' said Cashel.

'Yeah? What's your ax?'

'Tenor sax.'

'Really? Me too. That's what I used to play anyway. You heard of Iggy Pop?'

'You played with Iggy Pop?'

'Sure. Heartbreakers too. Nothing recorded

though, unfortunately. Mainly I played with a lot of bands you probably haven't heard of, round the early eighties. But I was making money, and I was sought after. Did some soundtrack work. Well, that's all over now, baby blue.'

'What happened to you?'

'I ain't really sure. Inthose last days of my humanity – round 1986, '87 – I was pretty fucked up. My fiancée left me and after that I took strongly to drinking and rock cocaine.'

'Why did your fiancée leave you? If you don't mind my asking.'

'Because I was drinking and smoking rock cocaine. Also she'd been my fiancée for a long time and she felt it was time we either got married or went our separate ways. I would've married her too, but even a little ceremony costs money and I was always spending my dough on . . . '

Mickey halted and stared up at the window.

'Drinking and rock cocaine?' Cashel tendered.

'I'm glad to see you were paying attention. So eventually I'm staggering home one night and these two cops drop the hook on me. Fortunately I hadn't smoked any rock that night but they still booked me on a D&D and threw me in the drunk tank. You ever been put in the drunk tank? No? Well, pray you never do. It's like the worst hospital you could imagine, with bars on the windows. They let you dry out there and you go crazy, start seeing things. Things worse than *me*. Like your loved ones coming back from the dead as vampires. It's scary and it's very depressing, when you realise you're all alone. So I was lying in bed and in a moment of clarity I prayed for the first time since I was a kid. I said, 'God – or whoever you are up there–

release me from this torment. I know I've wasted my life, my potential, but if you would just give me a hand here, I'll find some way to return the favour. Maybe you and I could get to be friends.' I knew that last remark was a little dumb the moment I said it, because I'm sure the Ruler of Heaven and Earth, Judge of All Men isn't short of friends, but I had to give it a shot. So I say this and wait a few minutes and nothing happens so I close my eyes and sigh and then – BAM! I'm sittin' at the counter of a bar in . . . Long Island, I think it was . . . feelin' great, thinkin' that everything is fine when I turn to make a sociable remark to the guy sitting next to me and the guy goes as white as winter, almost falls over himself getting out of there. So I'm wonderin' what that was all about and then I see myself in the mirror behind the bar and that answers *that* question.

'After that I found myself moved all over the world by some unseen hand. I never know where I'm going and when I'm *there* I have no fuckin' idea *why*. I'm not even sure about my corporeal state here – am I dead? Living? Reincarnated? What?

'What I *hope* is that this is just a transitional stage. You know? Like somehow I'm doin' the Almighty a favour, and when He feels I've paid my debt, He'll give me a break. But I don't know . . . '

Mickey went quiet for a bit and tapped a spindly leg on the carpet pensively.

'But I feel He's lookin' out for me. For instance, some people see me, but most don't. And the ones that see me are either alcoholic or borderline, so telling their friends there's a man-sized mosquito hangin' around ain't goin' to do them any favours and they know that, so they mostly keep quiet about it, which is a very good thing as far as I'm concerned. I can do without becoming the subject of a documentary.'

'So you're only visible to the lashed up?' asked Cashel. 'Like pink elephants?'

'Pink elephants?' Mickey repeated in disbelief. 'Fuck me. I guess there *are* worse things than being a giant mosquito. When did you see a pink elephant?'

'I didn't.'

'Good. You start seeing pink elephants you'll really *know* you've got a problem. By the way, I was admiring your boots. What are they, snakeskin? I really miss having good footwear. I miss having *feet* as a matter of fact. I miss playing my sax, I miss my fiancée – who ain't my fiancée *anymore*, of course – I miss New York City, I miss a lot of fuckin' things to tell ya the truth . . . Well . . . shit . . . I'm depressing myself here . . . I think I'm gonna take off. Would you mind if I had one more drink for the road?'

'Yeah, I do mind,' said Cashel. 'I'm sorry, Mickey, but I mind a hell of a lot.'

'Well, that's your prerogative I guess. Your blood sure tastes sweet though, like *Saaang-ga-ria!*' Mickey's wings started to buzz frenetically as he climbed to the broken basement window and started to lever himself through the gap.

'Where are you going?' asked Cashel.

'No idea, Marlon. That gets decided in flight. I hope it's somewhere humid. So long, pal!' he yelled, and buzzed off.

The next moment Cashel was looking up at a man of about thirty who made no impression on him other than he had an authentically concerned expression on his face.

'He's coming round,' he said loudly whilst looking at Cashel.

'Keep talking to him,' a woman's voice returned

from somewhere behind him. 'And spray him again with the vaporiser.'

The man crouching over Cashel held up a can.

'Don't worry, mate,' he said. 'It's just fizzy water,' and then he sprayed Cashel's face for about a minute with the contents of the vaporiser can. It was refreshing. He'd have to get himself one of those.

'The ambulance is on its way,' the woman said, and then she joined the man and they both stared at Cashel in a concerned way.

'I'm going to my room now,' said Cashel, getting off the floor. 'No, I don't need any medical attention, thank you. I'm sorry about your window. I'll pay for the damages.' He continued rambling as he found the hallway and fumbled with the latch on the door. 'Unless you're already insured. I hope you're insured. Household insurance is always a good . . . er . . . goodbye!'

He finished abruptly as the door opened and he made the short ascent back to his own front door. As he put his key in the lock, the ambulance pulled up behind him. He glanced over his shoulder at it, shuddered and got himself inside his house as swiftly as possible. He was lying on his bed with a damp tea cloth pressed to the gash on his head when there was a pounding at the door. Cashel hoped it would go away and after five minutes it did. People in his house spoke in tense and aggrieved voices for a while and then a few doors slammed and it was more or less quiet.

Perhaps I do need medical attention, thought Cashel before he fell asleep.

Cashel woke up the next day feeling and looking like a road accident. It was Sunday. He took a bus to the County Hospital on Eastern Road, got his cut stitched at the A&E and caught another bus home. Between waiting for buses and waiting for medical treatment, that used up most of the day. When he got home he found someone had eaten his falafel. He got himself wearily to the corner store and back, made himself four rounds of Welsh rarebit and drank a pot of tea, then called Evelyn.

'Evelyn, it's Cashel.'

'What do you want?'

'I want to say I'm sorry.'

'What for?'

'I can't remember. But I'm sorry anyway. I had an accident last night. I had to go to the hospital today. Otherwise I'd have called you earlier.'

'What happened?'

'I fell through a window.'

'What?!'

'I fell through a window. But I learned a valuable lesson from that. I'm going to stop drinking for a while – and another thing too . . . I want us to be together again. I mean the way we used to be.'

'Oh, Cashel.'

'Would you like to see a movie tonight? They're showing some psychedelic movie at the gallery. It's supposed to be a classic. It's only a couple of quid to get in. I'll buy the tickets.'

'Well, I've got Maple. Would they allow a dog in there?'

'I'm pretty sure they would. After all, it's a small and well-behaved dog.'

'He's a good dog,' said Evelyn defensively.

'He's a very good dog,' said Cashel, with all the sincerity he could gather.

'He's my baby,' said Evelyn in the same tone.

'He's my baby too,' said Cashel. He felt queasy but he thought it had sounded all right.

'What time does the film start?' asked Evelyn.

Cashel finished his call, hung up the phone and went to his room to smoke cigarettes and peruse the dictionary for unusual words until it was time to go out. He hoped the movie was good.

"The Pop Group's 'She is Beyond Good and Evil' is post-punk really, from the time when punk was getting a bit too clever-clever and danceable for its own good. I like the spiky DIY take on dancey wikkiwiki guitar licks and I like the lyrics, though I don't really think punk should do lyrics of this purple variety. Accepting the fact that The Fall are the only good post-punk band, then this song does show how bands were beginning to take punk into a new era. They had to discover synthesisers before they got any good. A couple of lines in the song fascinated me – 'Western values mean nothing to her' and, 'I'd exchange my soul for her.' It's all very femme fatale and doom laden and it's at the beginning of the era of intellectual lyrics in a punky setting (watch out, here come Scritti Politti, Wire, Gang of Four et al) which seemed appealing at the time, but doesn't now. The story I've written explores the idea of obsession as a viral disease."

She is Beyond Good and Evil

David Gaffney

Jeff didn't smoke, gave up years ago, but he missed the camaraderie, so when Luke invited him outside while he had a fag, Jeff quickly agreed, taking his cup of tea as something to do with his hands. The sun was scorching hot so they sheltered under a scrap of shade cast by the stunted birch sprouting from a crack in the pavement. Luke cupped a flame, put his cigarette to the fire and sucked smoke, while Jeff sipped tea, envying the sensuous curl of tobacco smoke from Luke's nostrils.

Luke began, in his low, searching, cigarette-scratched voice, to talk to Jeff about man stuff. Was Jeff a man of the world?

Some world, somewhere, Jeff supposed.

How many different women had Jeff shagged? Round figures, nothing specific. Had Jeff ever had sex in an office or work environment? In a toilet? Were there any sexual acts Jeff hadn't tried? How tall was the tallest woman Jeff had ever shagged? Who had been the most educationally qualified? What height had been the shortest girl? Who was the stupidest? The fattest?

Jeff replied in a careful, considered way and Luke nodded, pressing his lips together, saying, mmm, yes, I see, yet making no suggestions as to how Jeff might experience the same wild, untiring sex life as Luke, with its unending supply of differently shaped women from every social strata.

This part of his chat over, Luke butted out his cigarette on the concrete, ground it fiercely with his heel, lit another and, using the fag as a pointer, indicated a particular balcony on the new block of flats opposite. The new block had been thrown up in the past year and was a brutal collision of cones, spheres and rectangles ruining the line of the streetscape and rendering illegible the handsome neo-Gothic façade of the John Rylands library down the street. Jeff looked at the balcony indicated by Luke and, after a few moments, a young woman appeared wearing a dressing gown which, when she waved down at Luke, fell open, flashing a strip of milky skin. Inky short hair framed an impish face.

Luke waved back and the woman tossed her head defiantly, mimed pantomime laughter, then leaned on the balcony, smoking, looking down at them with a vulpine grin.

Luke told Jeff that the woman was Claire's mother. Claire was Luke's girlfriend. One thing Jeff was certain of: this young lady looked like nobody's mother.

Claire's mother went inside and reappeared with a dining table, which she placed on the balcony. She then produced a deckchair, which she lifted on to the table, positioning it carefully so that it wouldn't slide off, and she climbed onto the elaborate structure and sat down. This way she could view the city over the opaque glass screen that prevented residents tumbling off. It was, after all, the fifteenth floor.

Luke's face was glossy with sweat. He drew in a long draught of smoke, his cheeks sinking into deep hollows and a faint whistle coming from his teeth, then asked Jeff, through a smile shaped for and aimed at Claire's mother, if in Jeff's opinion it would be all right to see a mother and a daughter at the same time.

'What do you mean, see?'

'You know: see.'

Jeff looked up at Claire's mother. She was wearing headphones and her head twitched to and fro while her foot, dangling over the balcony rail, tapped a rapid beat in the air.

Jeff worried about whether he was getting into another pink/brown snooker ball scenario, which was, in his opinion, disgusting.

'I'm not sure, Luke,' Jeff said, secretly thinking that the last thing a man should do is betray his girlfriend with his girlfriend's mother. But then again, Jeff wasn't as experienced with women as Luke, so he kept this opinion to himself.

Luke had a sly way of smiling that allowed little wisps of cigarette smoke to escape from between his almost-closed lips, and he was doing that while he looked up at the woman on the balcony. He explained what he knew about the mother and daughter's relationship. It turned out they didn't get on. They'd had some row over the mother's last boyfriend, so there was hardly any contact between them. Luke knew this was the mother from pictures, and he knew she lived in this block. That's why he had begun to take his fag breaks on that side of the building. Curiosity. To see what she looked like, this ogre, this hated woman. As he explained this to Jeff, Luke became increasingly agitated. He abhorred the fact that Claire wouldn't even come to the phone when her own mother rang, and that letters with her own mother's handwriting on the envelope – her own mother's handwriting – went straight into the bin. But the main thing Jeff had to understand was this. Luke took a long, deep pull on his fag. He was developing a little thing for Claire's mother. More than little, really. He'd had a few drinks with her. And the woman had no idea that Luke was her daughter's boyfriend. Luke thought at first that he would just find out what the lady was like. Maybe try to get her and her mum back together. It wasn't right, a family split up like that. But after he'd met her a few times he forgot to mention about the daughter. And the more often he saw her, the more difficult it became to bring such a thing up. She had, Luke explained, these faraway eyes. He let this fact land, and neither of the men said anything for a long time. Luke pouted and exhaled smoke from the side of his mouth with a brusque malignance. They were both thinking about the faraway eyes.

Jeff looked up at the woman again. Long white legs on the balcony rail, slick with sun oil, glistening in the sun. Faraway eyes. Jeff wondered if there was a scientific explanation for faraway eyes.

Luke explained that he was by nature a big sharer, and he wondered if it was morally acceptable to allow the two women to share him. What did Jeff think? Should he do it?

'I'm not sure, Luke. It's going to have to be your call.'

'Have you ever done anything like that?'

'Not exactly like that, no'

'No. I guess not.'

Jeff thought privately that it would be simpler if Luke had started seeing the mother first. Then there would be no way even Luke could consider seeing the daughter, because she'd be like his stepdaughter. But the other way round? Jeff wasn't sure.

Luke read this thought.

'I mean, its not like I met the mother first. It's not like it's sick. Is it? I mean, is it? Is it sick, Jeff? That's what I need to know?'

'I really don't know, Luke.'

Claire's mum went inside and emerged again with a cocktail glass of green liquid, a red paper umbrella sticking out of it. She sipped audaciously, pinky finger cocked; Luke and Jeff were at work and she wasn't.

'Look at her. She is fucking gorgeous. Why is Claire so nasty to her?'

'Families,' Jeff said. 'It's like that sometimes.'

'She's like a mother-in-law, I suppose. And mother-in-laws are like stepmothers. They don't love like real mothers. Always evil.' Luke chucked his fag onto the ground and stamped it out. He seemed to be churning inside with unhappy lust. 'Everyone knows about stepmothers, Jeff. Or didn't you get fairy stories in that home?'

Luke waved up to Claire's mother, pointed at his wrist and mouthed *later*, then squeezed Jeff's shoulder roughly in his fingers, and said, 'Thanks for listening mate,' before disappearing inside.

Why did Luke always have to mention the home? Whatever Luke discussed with Jeff, *the home* ended up relevant in some way.

Jeff stayed to finish his tea and Claire's mother sat back more comfortably on her deckchair, crossed her legs, and allowed one slim foot to slip part way out of its sandal. She sipped her drink, tapped her toes, bopped her head.

Her mobile trilled and Jeff watched her reach down, pick it up and cradle it against her ear. She chatted happily for a time until abruptly she jerked up out of her seat and began to prowl the balcony, head shaking alarmingly, arms flinging this way and that, fingers jabbing at invisible enemies, mouth rattling staccato sentences into the phone. Jeff waited for something to happen.

Which it did. She screamed and tossed the phone off the balcony and it smacked against the concrete in front of him, fragments of metal and plastic spinning off. Then she heaved herself onto the balcony rail and sat astride it, wobbling drunkenly.

Jeff called out to her, but she didn't hear. Headphones on, she sat on the rail, swaying and gyrating, glass in one hand, fag in the other.

Should he call the police? Or Luke? The woman could plummet down at any moment and crack into the concrete, smashing into pieces like her phone. He called out again, but still no response. Maybe he was worrying unnecessarily. Maybe she did this sort of thing all the time. But he couldn't help thinking of her daughter Claire, and how, despite her mother's antics, she must surely love her really and how happy they both could be if Luke was somehow off the scene, and possibly there was a part for Jeff in all of this.

Then from Claire's balcony came a long impossible moan, whose sound had no word, and Jeff set off running, kicking a piece of broken mobile phone out of the way as he went.

Magazine really created their own subgenre of music, a propulsive post-glam punk rock which was mysterious, weird and threatening. 'I'm on the run from the outside of everything'–a perfect catch phrase riddled with angst and alienation. Chilling.

Shot By Both Sides

Lydia Lunch

Blood buckets down the undulating walls. Invisible fists rage with superhuman strength and hammer the door. The ancient wood frame buckles, crumples and heaves. The empty nursery reverberates with the mournful howl of a pitiful infant who cannot be located. I'm sitting cross-legged on the floor clutching my throat, trembling. Dry mouthed. Unable to breathe. *The Haunting of Hill House* is the most terrifying movie I've ever seen. I'm eight years old.

A suffocating humidity saturates the night air. Static electricity vibrates the hair follicles. The low buzzing hum of the black and white Motorola is swallowed up in the wheezing yelp of a stray dog, which bellows like a town crier somewhere in someone's backyard. His harried yapping immediately mimicked and amplified by every mutt in the neighbourhood in a round robin of barks and howls. A desperate warning cry which signals the coming maelstrom.

The atmosphere stiffens. The dogs retreat. Time bends. In a sudden explosion of white noise hundreds of frenzied voices come shrieking out of nowhere. As if all Hell's fury in a sudden expulsion from middle earth materialises, compounding my terror.

Men, women and children who have been hoisted upon the backs of older brothers, all shouting slogans in a demonic gospelled fervour. Equal work! Equal pay! Say it loud! We're black and we're proud!

The riots of 1967 have detoured down Clifford Avenue and are stampeding directly in front of my house. Hammers, baseball bats, pipes and bricks all employed in the demolition of cars, windows, storefronts. A hideous industrial opera of unbearable din. My father chain-smokes and paces. Unleashing a litany of curses. Punches the air in his best Marlon Brando as his station wagon crumbles under the endless battery of physical abuse. The ambulance and fire trucks barrel in, splitting the angry throng in two. Their sirens a deafening symphony which exaggerates the cacophony. Police helicopters circle the periphery. Giant mechanical insects whose diabolical hum blankets the shrill.

My fear is drowned in sound but reborn as joy in flames. The family car is set on fire. I start to laugh. Maniacally. To dance. To sing. 'Come on baby light my fire. Try to set the night on fire!!!!' My father assumes I've lost my mind and against my insistent protest sends me to my room.

I skulk upstairs dejected. 'If I had a hammer . . .' mumbled under my breath. A noisy rebellion of violence. Clanging. Pounding. Exciting. And I'm locked out! I can't really comprehend what's happening, but it feels so right. I'm no longer frightened, I'm charged up! Zoning in to the collective urgency. The passion. Determination. I head to the attic, my hidden retreat. Turn on the radio. Top 40 in 1967 was insane. Jefferson Airplane's homage to psychedelic drugs, 'White Rabbit', The Electric Prunes' 'I Had Too Much to Dream Last Night', Donovan's 'Season of the Witch', Wilson Pickett inviting you to take a chance and dance down dirty

Funky Broadway, 'The Marvelettes singing The Hunter Gets Captured by the Game', Jimi Hendrix with his sexy come on of 'Are You Experienced?' Back to back. I had no idea what any of these songs were referencing. What they really meant. How subversive they really were.

I used the radio to disappear. To escape from my family. Enter another dimension. Melt inside a psychedelic sound stage riddled with fantastic weirdos who were all creating something truly unique, which spoke directly about the times and how they were changing. I was transported by the soaring rhythms and strangled guitars which cascaded out through the airwaves and flooded me with a throbbing, slinky, soul-stirring music which I may have rejected as too traditional once I began making noise myself, but in retrospect so much of the music of the late 60s was experimental, diverse and full of radical statements which encouraged rebellion, liberation and sexual freedom. And no doubt had a great impact on my budding creativity.

'I wake up . . . in a cold sweat' stimulated me in ways I could only express by shaking my ass, flapping my arms and stomping my feet. Jimmy Lee Johnson, the seven-year-old black boy next door, 'Skinny legs and all', had the entire James Brown drop-to-one-knee-and-use-his-sweatshirt-as-a-cape routine off pat. It's the first time anyone flirted with me. I was amazed by his mimicry. His fluidity. His tiny body gliding through the air with so much passion and control. He must have caught JB on *The Ed Sullivan Show*. Everybody was glued to the tube on Sunday nights. The Rolling Stones. The Animals, George Carlin, all penetrated my unformed psyche, courtesy of Mr Sullivan. Even the infamous Doors controversy, where

Morrison refused to change 'I knew we couldn't get much higher', subsequently banning him from future appearances, struck a raw nerve in my adolescent conscious.

Music is the connective tissue between protest, rebellion, violence, sexual awareness and community. Just the way it is. The Summer of Love. What a bold-faced lie! Reagan was elected Governor of California. Lyndon B Johnson increased troop presence in Vietnam, ignoring the massive demonstrations, which rocked the nightly news. 70,000 strong in New York City alone. Race riots stormed through Cleveland, Detroit, Watts, Birmingham, Alabama, Rochester, New York and hundreds of other US cities, inflaming tensions. Muhammad Ali was stripped of his World Heavyweight Championship for refusing the draft. Carl Wilson of the Beach Boys wouldn't go to war either and got tied up in a five-year legal battle, which he eventually won. The Boston Strangler was sentenced to life in prison and escaped from the institution he was held in.

Bread was 22 cents a loaf, a gallon of gas was 28 cents and the inner city ghetto which I called home was brimming with hard-working people with attitude and conviction whose lust for life couldn't be beaten out of them by piss-poor housing conditions, lousy pay, the police or politicians. They taught me to fight for what I believed in, take pride in what I did, never give up, keep the faith and, when hoping for a better tomorrow isn't enough, to turn up the goddamn music and dance the blues away.

1967 helped to define who I was to become. I may have been too young to fully grasp the political implications of the time, but it started a fire in my belly that burns as bright today as it ever did. The National Organization of Women was officially incorporated in '67. Grace Slick and Janis Joplin both threw down at the Monterey Pop festival. Shirley Temple ran for congress. I was just a tiny terror screaming my bloody head off to 'Funky Broadway', already plotting my big city escape.

© Ferry Gouw

The KKK Took My Baby Away

Dev Hynes

I was awake again. I could tell I was for sure this time.

I had figured out the last three moments of consciousness were mere fragments of the part of my brain not frozen numb with a throbbing, extremely painful fear.

I rested my head upon the sharp metal corner of the front left window, trying to recall the twisted events that led me to this most unlikely of circumstances and with each road I revisited in my brain, the more I pushed my head into the corner of the cold window frame.

Ever since The Fuxzprator Regime gained control nearly thirty years ago now, no one in the whole of Bazatof had felt safe.

The Fuxzprator Regime is led by a tall, slim, young man who goes by the name of H. He has a jet-white head of short, slicked-back hair, a pale face and dark, cutting, sunken-in eyes.

A glossy headshot of H is plastered on the walls all around Bazatof, and at the fourth minute of every seventeenth hour we must kneel down at the nearest picture and mutter the almighty prayer of H. If we don't, we lose the next sixteen hours, as in, they are erased, gone. Within a blink of an eye, you're standing outside of a Fuxzprator station, knowing you have but an hour to find another head shot to kneel down too. With each time you're caught, they add another hour, plus the previous hours. So first time, 16 hours; second time, 33 hours; third time, 51 hours.

It's a ludicrous concept and I've yet to grasp its relevance.

No one seems to know much about H. Or remember the first time they even heard of him or even when they voted him into power. It just happened. But we grow more used to it with each passing day. It's normal to wake up one day and have a new building fully erected across the road from your apartment. Such things are never questioned.

But I read. *I* read the stories of the old world, and I know that things took time. I know buildings take years to be made, for people to be inside, to be working . . .

The only constant I seem to have in my life is my family.

I'd do anything for them.

My wife is dead.

The woman I love is dead.

The woman I wanted to spend the rest of my life with is dead.

For reason's unbeknownst to us an alien race called the Krahpatilt Kequa Konsalant (KKK for short) had been watching our planet for some time. I'm aware that I'm skimming over a lot of details, but please understand the torment I'm going through right now. The KKK had been watching our 'fair' (fear) planet for some time now and I'm going to assume they must've had an ongoing feud with H.

I wish I knew the answers. I'm in a tiny space pod, crunched inside, speeding through space to what I think might be the planet of the Krahpatilt Kequa Konsalant. But I have no way to be sure until I arrive. It was the only vehicle I could find. I need some answers. My wife, my beautiful Lindsay, was taken away from me forever. And my son, Jacob. Why must this happen?

I have no one.

I look outside this capsule and all I see is space.

I see black.

I should've given up. Will I even make it to this planet? And when I get there, is it even going to be where I need to be?

They took my son away from me. Just snatched him from my arms. Why my son?

I was in the wrong place as always.

Am I making sense? My mind is racing. I'm skipping subjects. The point of writing this down is so that . . . what is the point?

Oh God . . . what am I doing?

OK . . . I think maybe a day has just passed since I wrote that last sentence. I can't work out if my clock works fine, or if it tends to stop from time to time.

From time to time is an interesting phrase . . .

Technically I guess that would mean constantly right? As we are actually moving from time to time all the time . . .

Or does it tend to stop constantly?

That would possibly suggest it's just stopped altogether . . . and never continues . . . so I'd be stuck in time.

Which is precisely how I feel right now.

What's the time?

Well it's actually an irreversible non-spatial

continuum from the past through the present onwards t'wards the future . . .

I feel like shit. I wonder how long I was out for this time.

I dreamt of Lindsay. I dreamt of the moment they took her away from me. I dreamt of the look in her eyes before she was liquefied by that Krahpatilt Kequa Konsalant scumbag. I should have done something. I didn't do anything.

I didn't do anything.

I froze.

I deserve whatever torment comes my way, but Jacob? What did he ever do?

I was still frozen to the spot when they grabbed him and exited the apartment through the window.

It may feel like I've summed up the most horrifying moment of my life rather quickly. But that's how it was . . . and that's how it is . . . it happened quickly, there was no time to think, no time to question motives, no time to think about what's right and wrong . . . and I am soulless now because of this.

But I will get you back, Jacob. I promise you. I will get you back, and the Krahpatilt Kequa Konsalant will all pay, with every ounce of my aching body I will make them suffer plights of which they have never ever suffered before.

I'm thirsty.

I didn't think this through.

What is H doing right now?

Maybe he got taken in by the KKK . . . maybe they're torturing him right now. I hope they destroy him, it's his fault, I know this for a fact . . . his giant golden face being smashed to pieces by a . . .

What the hell is that?

OK, so I just looked outside the window. I think I can see the Planet of the KKK . . . I predict two more days roughly until I arrive . . .

Question: What's the difference between a Krahpatilt Kequa Konsalant resident and a Bazatofian?

Answer: The Krahpatilt Kequa are *Konsalant*-ly annoying!!!!

HAHAHAHAHAHHAHAHAHAHHhahahahHAHAH hhahahHhahahhHAHAHAHAHhahahahahhHAHAH hahhHAHHAHAHhahahhahHAHAHhahhahahahHh ahahhHAHHhahhahahHhahahahhHAHAHAHHAhh ahaah . . .

Time for more sleep.

Check list upon arrival at the Krahpatilt Kequa Konsalant planet:

1. Kill every Krahpatilt Kequa Konsalantian I see.
2. Keep one alive to show me where my son is.
3. Find food.
4. Find drink.
5. Remember where space pod is.
6. Find back-up space pod.
7. Find weapon.
   Wait, I think I've written these in an awful order.

I need a new brain.

Hello, if you'll please humour me.

I shall refer to the first book of the *Cosmic Trigger Trilogy*.

Cosmic Trigger I: The Final Secret of the Illuminati by Robert Anton Wilson teaches us a few things:

1. Self-induced brain change is, indeed, very possible. I shall look into this in a second.

2. Reality is definitely subject to change in the eye of the beholder.

I need to find my reality tunnel. As long as I stay on that path, nothing can go wrong, nothing. I have crushed the old filters of Bazatof and am now building new walls within this pod. I am very aware of the confirmation biases of which I am setting myself up for right now, but I also believe because of the situation I'm in right now . . . I am allowing myself this little taste of inductive inference.

Was Leo Tolstoy an idiot?

It was he who said, 'The most difficult subjects can be explained to the most slow-witted man if he has not formed any idea of them already; but the simplest thing cannot be made clear to the most intelligent man if he is firmly persuaded that he knows already, without a shadow of doubt, what is laid before him.' Wait, but maybe that means that I'm the 'slow-witted man'. That is more likely than a nineteenth-century Russian theorist being a fool.

Oh Christ . . . I am standing at the gates of Hell and looking straight into the eyes of Morton's Demon . . . there are too many overlays . . .

I seem to be getting closer to the planet whilst

simultaneously becoming the LIMP in the LAMP.

I'm worried now. I seem to be losing my mind. I'm neither hungry nor thirsty anymore. Every part of my body is pulling me towards this planet.

We're so close, we're getting faster now. I can see the planet, it's glowing, and the sparkling red beauty is filling my heart and stomach, both of which are racing and spinning. My breathing is going out of control.

I'm sweating a lot . . . this must be the planet, this can only be the planet . . . surely . . . I see nothing else now.

Just red, such a bright vibrant blaze . . . my eyes are widening . . . this is it . . . I feel the capsule speeding more and more . . . my hair is starting to fall out . . . I can see it shedding . . . I'm going to cover my face with my hands.

How do you define punk? I dunno. I just wish that every 19-year-old could feel as empowered as I did when I first saw the Clash in 1977

Revolution Rock

Billy Bragg

Seeing The Clash at the Rainbow Theatre in London in May 1977 answered the conundrum that had troubled me since adolescence: how was a kid from Barking, who wasn't pretty and couldn't sing very well and who had no idea of how the music industry worked, going to make it as a rock star? Up until that moment, my best guess had been to conform to the prevailing fashions of the day: dress like the rock-star-next-door Peter Frampton ('The Face of '76' according to *Sounds*), write songs about girls and summer and hope that someone noticed me.

It took The Clash to show me the way.

Conformity won't get you noticed, punk – confrontation is the quickest way to get people's attention. You're not pretty? So what? Show the world you don't care by putting a safety pin through your cheek to making yourself even more unsightly. Can't sing? Who cares? It's what you are singing about that matters. Don't understand the workings of the music industry? Well, don't worry, we're going to turn that world upside down.

Most important of all, don't wait for someone to come along and do it all for you. Do It Yourself.

This DIY ethic was the central tenet of punk. It cut us free from complacency and consumerism, empowering us to create. And it came with its own manifesto: The music industry will no longer dictate what records get released – you will decide because you will make them!

The music papers will no longer dictate what is good or bad – you will decide because you will write your own fanzines!

Fashion designers will no longer dictate what you wear – you will decide because you will develop your own style!

Old farts will no longer patronise you with their hippy ideals – you will decide what is right and what is wrong because you are the future!

By taking control of the means of production of music, magazines, shirts, shoes and trousers – all the things that were important to us – we were going to change the world.

More than any other band, The Clash seemed to embody these ideals, although, in a sense, they were merely doing what all good artists do – mirror the concerns of their audience. But we didn't want to be mirrored, we wanted to be led and where The Clash went, we followed. When, two weeks before the ANL/RAR Carnival Against the Nazis, they were added to the bill, we knew we had to be there too.

My political sympathies at the time chimed with the RAR ideal. When me and my band mates had gone into the studio to make a demo tape in March 1977, one of the four tracks we recorded was a cod-reggae song that I had written called 'Rivers of Blood', which sought, in a clumsy yet sincere way, to refute Enoch Powell's vision of a race war on the streets of Britain.

There is a big difference, however, between writing about a struggle and standing up to be counted. Attending the Carnival Against the Nazis was the first political event I ever took part in and it was, in its way, as significant as seeing The Clash at The Rainbow.

The organisers had been expecting around 20,000 – the number of RAR badges they'd sold in the previous twelve months – but on arrival in Trafalgar Square, it became clear that the turnout was massive. While the NF marched beneath their ranks of union Jacks, we set off beneath Union banners, yellow ANL roundels and punk pink RAR stars. The six miles to Victoria Park were covered in high spirits. 10,000 whistles had been handed out and we all took turns on the megaphone to lead chants of, 'The National Front is a fascist front! Smash the National Front.'

En route to the East End, the march wound its way through the financial district where only months before I'd been working as a messenger of a merchant bank; Cheapside, where I used to kill time in Revolver Records listening to the latest releases on Stiff Records; Princes Street, where I worked; up Threadneedle Street past the Bank of England and then up broad Bishopsgate towards Shoreditch and the East End.

There had been talk of trouble – the last big anti-NF demo had turned into a riot when a crowd of 5,000 anti-fascists had refused to allow the NF to march through Lewisham in August 1977 – but we never encountered any opposition.

All I can remember seeing is one little old man in a flat cap, standing, beer in hand, outside a pub near the top of Brick Lane, giving the Nazi salute to the passing marchers. Perhaps he was the last of Oswald Moseley's blackshirts, reduced to making a futile gesture in the face of this massive show of strength by the anti-fascist movement.

When we finally reached Hackney, it became clear that the event had vastly exceeded expectations. An estimated 100,000 people had converged on Victoria Park, one person in opposition for every vote that the NF had won in the London council elections the year before.

The Clash were not top of the bill that day, their late addition meaning that they would have to go on mid-afternoon. They delivered a short, sharp set of favourites from their first album along with a few new songs like 'Tommy Gun'. From the reaction of the crowd, it was clear that most of us had come to see The Clash. Whatever followed would surely be an anti-climax, but the crowd did not disperse, staying to hear sets from joint headliners Steel Pulse and The Tom Robinson Band. Both had been staunch supporters of RAR during its first year, appearing at several gigs.

Steel Pulse were reggae rockers from Birmingham whose current hit was their chilling anti-racist anthem, 'Ku Klux Klan'. The Tom Robinson Band was led by a singer who stood out even in those days of stand-out personalities.

The first out gay pop singer who didn't dress like an alien, Tom oozed normality, not even bothering to cut his curly shoulder-length locks to meet the strict regulations that punk had imposed on hairstyles. He looked as affable as your best mate and dressed like him too. His homosexuality was not made palatable by being hidden behind a veil of androgyny, nor was it lightened by camp. Tom was gay and out and angry. And incredibly brave.

In 1978 you could get your head kicked in if someone thought you were a 'queer'. Homosexuality was a taboo subject, even for the punk audience. Having had a top-five hit in late 1977 with the anthemic '2-4-6-8 Motorway', a song extolling the overwhelmingly straight activity of truck driving, he followed it up with 'Sing if You're Glad to Be Gay', a bitter, ironically titled song which expressed to the straight audience how badly gays were treated by society in general and by the police in particular.

When The Tom Robinson Band sang the song at Victoria Park, a strange thing happened. All of the men who were standing near me and my friends began singing along with gusto and kissing each other passionately on the lips. Turning around, we were aghast to find that we had spent much of the gig standing under a huge banner that said 'Sing if You're Glad to Be Gay'.

Somewhat embarrassed, we shuffled away as politely as we could.

Having grown up in Barking, I'd never encountered an 'out' gay man before. I wasn't so much shocked as puzzled. What were these gays doing at a Rock Against Racism gig? Surely the day was all about black people, wasn't it?

Eventually, the penny dropped: just as Hitler didn't only target the Jews, the fascists were against anyone who was in any way different from their narrow definition of society. Blacks, Asians, gays, lefties, punks – we were all inferior as far as the NF were concerned. From that day onward, I knew what I needed to do if I wanted to oppose the forces of conservatism – be as different from them as possible, celebrate that difference and stand together in solidarity with whomever they targeted.

The first ANL/RAR Carnival was a watershed, setting the tone for the decade to come. Those of us who were there that day would go on to support the Two Tone movement, the miners, CND, anti-apartheid, Nicaragua, Red Wedge, the GLC, Live Aid. It was the moment when my generation took sides.

It was also The Clash's greatest moment. Although they undoubtedly did better gigs, the context of their performance seemed to fulfil the hopes that they had raised. The Clash sealed their myth as rock's greatest rebels on that Sunday afternoon, nailing their ragged colours to the mast of political pop forever. However, the pressures of trying to live up to the expectations of their audience would prove their undoing.

In the heady days of punk, I believed that The Clash were going to change the world – which was foolish of me, because they were only a rock 'n' roll band. Unfortunately for them, The Clash also believed this as well, which was foolish of them, too.

That they didn't bring civilisation to its knees by playing loud and fast polemical songs does not detract from the lasting effect they had on the lives of those of us who were willing them to succeed. When my turn came to come up with actions to match the political sentiments of my songs, the lessons I learned from The Clash's mistakes were invaluable.

Their failure to engage with mainstream politics was central to my decision to work closely with the Labour Party in the hope of defeating the Tories in the 1987 election. The sad realisation that The Clash's politics were often little more than a pose forced me to overcome any fears of being seen as 'uncool' and take the flak I attracted for founding the Labour-supporting collective of musicians and artists known as Red Wedge in 1985.

The Clash's failure to change the world helped me to keep my own role in perspective. I realised early on in my career that the responsibility for changing the world lies not with the performer but with the audience. To suggest otherwise would be the worst kind of charlatanism, excusing the audience from any responsibility for making the world a better place.

What a performer can do, however, is bring people together for a specific cause, to raise money or consciousness, to focus support and facilitate an expression of solidarity. Which is precisely what The Clash did in Victoria Park for Rock Against Racism. Before I saw the hundred thousand like-minded souls gathered that day, I was reluctant to oppose the casual racism that I'd heard at work. The realisation that I was not the only person who hated what the NF stood for gave me the courage to speak out against the racists and homophobes.

The Clash taught me a valuable lesson that day, which I have in the back of my mind every time I write a song or step out onto a stage: although you can't change the world by singing songs and doing gigs, the things you say and the actions you take can change the perspective of members of the audience.

The Clash brought me to RAR, Tom Robinson introduced me to the politics of sexuality and those brave gay men with their big pink banner made me realise that we were all on the same side. And although the world was just the same as I travelled home on the tube that evening, my perspective of it had been changed forever.

action time and vision

(being a true story of punk rock glastonbury and pogles wood)

Billy Childish

we'er waighting around on the old unmade road out front of the art college, full of pot holes stuffed with busted bricks, lumps of flint and any old junk they could find bunged in there.

punk rock happened quite quick, then it was over . . . there were a few bits left but mostly it was over. id been listning to buddy holly befor, then the jam's 2nd single had a colour sleeve and a brand new type of idiot was born who thort that the boom town rats were an actual punk rock group, then paul weller was telling people to vote consevative, so that was the end of that.

along thru the cherry blossoms of new road comes this old bus wobbling on busted springs. it pulls up the dirt road, the doors wheeze open and out jumps this girl who hikes up her skirts and pisses rite there infront of us. it seams in my mind now that she had strippy stockings on and a hot, firey energy propelled by drugs. she aimed it rite up against the back wheel.

a load more long hairs climb down the 3 worn steps, then some hurberts with short hair. 2 of them carrying guitar cases. i whatch them cearfully as they pass by and off up the side of the building. a little stream of piss is creeping towards me thru the dust and forms a puddle round my bumper boots. the bus has got an empty destination roller, dirty windows and stained orangy-yellow curtens. it lookt pretty rusted-up for pop stars.

i cut up round the front of the building and pass a certain singer with cropt hair and small eyes arranged either side of his hooter. he is sat on a wall batting the breeze with a little fellow who appears to be wearing perjarmers and his nans table cloth. the little fellow dosnt have much hair on top but makes up for it by hanging a few strings down the back. much like a bald tree that has been parshially infested with catipillers.

as i too am in a group i slow my pace as i pass and notcholently raise my hand in a gesture of brotherly acknowlagment, as if we'er equels. the certain singer chirps 'hellow' at me. once out of site i sit breathless behind the wall.

its a fine and exciting thing to be in a punk rock group, to have credentials, to be able to look girls in their lying eyes, as if to say 'i too am special, certainly more special than your ridiclious boyfriends, and maybe one day, in the impossible futcher, you will regret not marrying me and for thinking me ugly.'

the stage is marrooned down one end of the carpark. it has its own force; a strange energy; at once compelling and inviting, yet also somehow overblown and mocking.

lucky for us the hippys still hold sway in the world. naturally they are stoned and useless, and by and large their days as a distinct race are numbered but they are the next best thing to grown ups that we've got, and thru their dedication, so stands the stage.

yes, hugh the hippy with his dirty straw coloured curles organised borrowing that pile of old sticks – iluminated by coloured lites – from canterbury college. and hugh the hippy with his greecy rotting bellstaff jacket, rang his contacts on the london squat scean and got these idiots down here to play for us. further to this it was hugh the hippy who single handedly organised chucking these bales of straw on the harsh tarmack, thereby providing seating for us and the impending audience. and of course it was hugh the hippy, smoking his big eligal ciggerets, who blagged this half busted p.a. for us to sing thru.

we drink from cans of stout.

technickly we are still children and as such it is our role to go on and play 1st.

'1-2-3-4 !'

hippy hippy shake. it really is strange to be scrutenised by those below. to be the eppycenter of all their eye balls: girls eyes, mens eyes. gray eyes, blue eyes, green eyes, eyes that have seen all manner of inexplicable sites yet somehow, from up here, seam quite blind.

acutally im just doing as im told: singing a song i heard played on nanna lewis gramerphone sometime in 1963. mother was dancing with me, flinging me round the room. and now i wear that same nylon top she was wearing back then, the one with the orange and blue hoops.

next its the turn of the long hairs with the pissing girl playing a screeching violin accompanied by strange banshie-like shrieking from her open mouth.

gradually darkness fills up the car park. the hippys depart the stage and the main group assend in their place. we see their faces as if lit by distant burning villages.

when seeing someone you admire it is impossible not to compare inadqueses and have all manner of feeling which are hard to pin down precisely, and in retrospect some of those impressions grow hard to remember, and if remembered at all remain still quite difficult to effectively describe.

'1-2-3-4 !'

i didnt know they were counting in the timing, i thort it was just a quaint afectation. then everything starts clattering. quite a din. a small child wouldnt put up with it, nor an adult for that matter but to our ears it has a certain urgent energy that mirriors our discomfort with peace and harmony and lifes lack of real war, even thou we are of course timid by education.

after the sounds have ecoed into nothing i sit exhorsted amongst the straw bales, which are actually quite itchy and not the best designed furniture ever. hugh the hippy lites one of his cigerets and the certain singer, who is near by, walks over chirps 'hello' again and takes a very deep puff. i feel his small eyes looking at me out of the darkness and his voice is inviting us to come play with him and his friends at a free festivel near glastonbury town this week end.

the car belongs to our guitarist who has 2 eyes, both of them bulgy. our slow minded bass player and a girl called vennessa head also travels with us. venessa is ritly named because she does in fact own a large, square shaped head.

we are crammed into the back of an ancient carpri, our arses perched on a narrow hard, shelf which could only charitably be called a seat. the other advantage is that the roof sloaps down at such an acute angle that your head is hammered down on every bump in the road and your face is thrust into the seat in front.

we follow hugh the hippy, who drives an old blue transit, weaving thru the early morning traffic. little russ, our drummer, the postgate twins and a girl with fat legs from deptford are on board.

how splended to be on the open road!

of course we race with the van. only being held on with bungy clips the wings of the capri pound like pile drivers. finnaly the dial reads 90 mph, at which point there is a loud bang and a great plume of purple smoke rockets down the duel carrage way behind us. we pull into a layby till the van catches up then poodle out after hugh, knocking along at 40, the engin rattling like a tin of nails. truth is this '63 capri is a derilict rust buckit.

nite time we come to an old ww2 bomber station and try to kip in the car. its quit lumpy on the back seat. at home you can stretch your legs out fairly easerly and we actually have curtens, matrices and matching pillows. but the colour of the car at least is pleasing – a washed-out dusty yellow.

about 2 or 3 in the morning i give up trying to sleep and clamber over the front seat to escape into the icy nite. i walk round the car 7veral times befor curling up on the old run way. my teeth are chattering like casternets. it really seams i should have brought a comfortable sleeping bag, or at least some sort of coat or jacket. the frost makes quite an interesting patten in the early morning lite and i bang my head on the exhorst pipe. if you stop to listen you can hear the guitarist sawing wood in the car above.

theres the smell of frying bacon and muffeled voices coming from the van, so i hobble over and try to look in the back windows. it takes several loud bangs on the the doors before the giggling stops and they acknowlege me.

'what?'

'its me.'

'yes, it is.'

'can i come in?'

'we'cr a bit bissy, can you come back later'

'its frezzing out here'

'come back in 10 minits'

'i dont know how long that is.'

'look at your watch.'

'i havent got one'

'fucking hell!'

the door opens a crack and a sumptious, greecy warmth rushes out and hits me in the mug.

i peep in there. the postgate twins, our drummer, little russ and the fat leg'd bird from deptford are all ensconsed on an old pink mattrice, whilest hugh the hippy makes a brew on a portable gas stove. theres a jet of blue flame and all of them are woofing down bacon sandwiches. i watch the bread dissappering into their mouths – crusts and all.

to be fair and honest, i probably cant remember any of the details properly and it is quite possible that i was allowed to sit on the corner of their precious, pink matrice. and who knows maybe one of them may even have offered me a sip of their tea, thou to be perfectly honest i can remember no such occurrence.

it also transpires that the twins have a full size tent in there but couldnt be bothered putting it up on account that are were quite comfortable already.

i dont know which way we went or how we got there but we sit in the window of a café to whatch the lorrys go by on the big road.

theres a surving lady who has teeth that stick out so flat you could eat your bacon and eggs off them. she brings tea. i peer into mine which has the colour and taste of oxtail soup.

we drink up and are just getting back on the road when little russ comes scurrying across the carpark with his trousers half down, tucking himself in.

'in the cars, quick' he shouts, then the surving lady comes galloping out after him, really showing her teeth.

'you disgusting little pervert!'

she's shouting at little russ. its him she hates. he visted the ladys toilets on account that the gents was stuffed up and overflowing with shit.

'all of you, you perverted creatures!'

we look at her curiously then a lorry driver starts walking towards us adjusting his ciggeret in his mouth and rolling up his shirt sleeves. Quick as you like we jump in the cars and motor off.

the roads wind on and on.

i tell you this much – they've got some hedges down that way.

we pass occasional broken down busses and police road blocks. 7everal times we'er sent back the way weve come by policmen chewing on bits of straw and talking in slow slured voices, like pirets. hugh says that they all have webbed fingers and toes.

gradually, bit by bit, we seam to be spireling towards our destination.

. . . we come to a track. we pass in under the trees, which stretch out their arms above us for mile after mile.

theres fresh tyer tracks and a clearing . . . a couple of rotting teepees over there, like smoking wizards hats.

actually, we wake up the inhabitents and are surrounded by wild faced children. their hair is tangled like street urchins and they wear no shoes. i climb out and take a deccas about, still bent double. they peer up at me with pinched, hungry faces.

up the other end of the field, just vissable thru the mud, is a pile of palets with a half collapsed tarpauling slung over them like a hammock but full of pond water. thats the stage.

theres no sign of atv or the pissing girl.

the chief wizard comes out his tent and tells hugh theres been no groups here since wednesday. 'since the generator broke down.'

hugh trades some petrol for a bag of rice and then we jump back in the motors and pull away, turning in the thick mud and heading back the way we came. the weels spin, the engin knocking like a whore house.

the raggedy children stair after us, their big sauser eyes shinning and bubbles of green snot sucking from their noses. the wizard raises his staff, then his gone thru the trees

as far as fields go this is a good one. it has its own owls ghoasting about, white thru the mist, and a little stream set way back of the road. we lite a fire and rustle up some grub: beans and sausages and a ½ loaf. the bag of salt has busted open and hugh tells me to go chuck it behind the bushes. the food is quite edible, thou you dont get a second helping and theres no pudding.

i go dangle my feet in the icy stream.

theres some deers eating grass up the way. being of an artist is temprement i make some drawings then its time to kip.

we all help the postagate twins set up their grand marquee then crawl in on our hands and knees to curl up in the damp.

i wake up freezing. its gray, not lite or dark, then

a policeman sticks his big face in thru the flaps. i recognise him as a policman because of his hat with the shining badge.

we all have to get up, weather we'er still tired or not and go on parade outside. the fires gone out. its hard to belive that those cold gray ashes were dancing with lite only moments ago.

we'er lined up, counted, then lead back across dew soaked grass with one officer leading and another guarding the rear.

all the way across the field i watch lisa with the fat legs flicking little blue pills over the heads of the policman. they scatter into the long grasses and gossomer webs. lisa says she knows that idiot out of squeeze with the piano: which is just another fake punk rock group.

theyve got a nice shinny black moria parkt out on the road waighting for us and a sergeant with walrus like flesh hanging round his neck loads us in, bangs the doors shut and climbs in front. we watch the country side disappearing away from us.

you come thru some fields and theres a small town with a horse trough at one end and a tree growing up the other. we drive along the little high street and pull in round the back of the police station, where they let us out and march us into the building.

theres a neon lite in there and we all have to stand in front of a white wall and hold up little signs with our names on whilst they take our mug shots. it smells of boild caulflowers in there. then they ink up our fingers, steal our belts and laces and sling us in the clink for the afternoon.

the idear, according to the walrus sergeant, is that we should all confess to drug smugling. i empty the fluth out of my pockets.

my asproes are confiscated rite off.

what a pack of devils!

the head gets her own woman pc to frisk her. the head has quite a small voice and is studying fashion, if it is really possible to study such a thing.

over the next few houres we are taken to the interview room, one by one, to admire the asperdesta they've got growing in there. I cant help but notice that the pot is plastic.

you have to sit at this gray desk with your hands on top 'in clear view' whilest the walrus skinned sargent shouts at you. then you get a cup of tea and are soothed by the musical tones of the sandy haired pc (constable merryworth) whos main claim to fame is having mossy looking tuffts sprouting from his ear holes. then its the turn of the walrus sergeant to shout at you again.

apparently he pushed one of the twins heads into the wall of the cell.

its getting towards evning when all the doors are unlockt and we are finnaly let out our cells and led into the charge room.

the walrus sargent is sat with a pile of junk retrived from the camp site arranged neatly on the desk in front of him.

it seams that the only real evedence they can rustle up is an ancent ½ smoked 'big ciggaret' constable merryworth found rattling around in the bottom of the eldists twins coat pocket.

the sargent holds it up to the lite bulb, turning it over and over between his thick fingers, that look for all the world like short stubby toes.

'so! . . . have you seen that! that's something.'

he strokes his hooter. 'my oh my, what have we got

here then, lover! your sweet treet for later, is it? you scum!'

clearly he is over the moon. he looks down and reads the charge sheet in front of him, his lips moving slightly.

'so your name really is . . . postgate?'

'yes'

the sergeant amends something on the charge sheet.

'your father wouldnt be oliver postgate, by any chance?'

'yes, he would.'

'thee oliver postgate. who did the clangers tv show?'

'thats him'

'and the soup dragon?'

'yes.'

'and bag puss . . . and noggin the nog?'

the twins nod as one. 'do you here that, constable meryworth. we have celebritys in our midst.'

constable merryworth grins his thick looking lips. 'and pogels wood.' he adds

the walrus sergeant looks at constable merryworth sturnly and turns back to the twins

'well under the circumstances i think we can forget this little matter . . . steven.' and he drops the afending 'ciggaret' into the the gray metal bin by his feet and dusts his hands.

'but as for you', and he turns to face me, 'im sending these off for analasis,' and he holds up my little packet of aspros.

'but their aspros.'

the sergeant survays me doubtfully. his silver-grey coloued eyes are flectd with 3 gold dots.

'thats what they all say. isnt that rite, constable merryworth.'

'yes, sargent.'

the walrus nods his head. 'yes, sargent.'

'but their still in their foil' i explain, trying to point to the packet, which he keeps just out of my reach.

'thats as may be, young man . . .'

'and theyve got aspro impressed on all the tablets.'

'look, no ones pulling the wool over my eyes, lover. ive seen it all before!'

and he tosses the packet back on the desk.

'and now theres the little matter of a highly suspicious subtance that one of my dutifull offices retrieved from the camp site. correct, constable merryworth.'

'absoluty correct, sargent.' and constable merryworth passes the the remnents of the bag of salt, re-rappt in a cellophain bag, to the waighting hand of the walrus.

'where did you find this item constable?'

'i found this on inspection of the imidiat fauner ajoining the location of the illisit trespass, and belive the contents to be cocain, sargent.'

'cocain,' repreats the walrus sergeant, musicly.

'thats never cocain' mutters hugh the hippy.

the sergeant looks at him, with the expression of a sulky old woman

'it is if i say it is. lover!'

'if i could afford that much cocain i wouldnt be dumping it behind a bush!

'so you do admits to hiding it behind a bush! rite that down, contable merryworth. the defendant admits to hiddin itiems behind a bush!'

merryworth takes his note book from his breast pocket and dutifully rites it down, word for word.

'excuse me,' i venture 'you could just taste it.'

the sergeant looks at me coldly. 'to check if it is table salt or not, i mean.'

the sergeant narrows his eyes. 'oh no! . . . no, no, no! i'm not falling for that one, lover. im not getting addicted!'

Afterword: Spiral Scratch

John Robb

Choosing your favourite punk single is an impossible task. Each three-minute rush comes so loaded with meaning and cheap thrills that it's become a part of my life. Every salvo, every breathlessly sneered lyric, every battered record sleeve . . . what were once thrilling bulletins from an imagined teenage wasteland are now like ragged antiques from a distant history. Where once I flicked through them like they were fast-forwarding to the future, I come to them now like an archaeologist searching for meaning in this scrapbook of youthful kicks.

Not that this has diminished their power. They still sound as exciting as when I first played them, they still have that strange rush of honesty and yearning that they ever had. They are classics and now I have to pull just one out of the pile.

Punk was the high watermark of the seven-inch single – the ultimate pop artifact. You had one song to make your statement and then get outta here. The whole period is littered with fantastic releases and as I flick along a creaking shelf stacked with battered records, I'm lost.

The Xerox riff onslaught matched the cut-and-paste artwork of the sleeves. Cover art had arrived at the same time as punk and became a key part of the whole movement. It may not have been invented by the punk bands, but punk made the whole concept its own. Its furious invectives were matched by the guerrilla collage that had been taught at art school in the 70s, and suddenly they had a place to exist and thrive.

So I digress, somehow there has to be a Number 1 single in this huge pile of vinyl. Some days for me it could be The Clash's thrilling incitement to live! To exist! To feel! Or it could be the Sex Pistols' power-chorded, anarchic, holy barbarism. It could be the dank, dark punk Floydism of The Stranglers with that killer bass sound. It could be the bright, shiny, punk pop of Generation X. It could be X-Ray Spex with their sax -driven anthems and genius lyrics by Poly Styrene. It could be Crass and their revolutionary missives from beyond the frontline. It could be The Fall's thrilling rough and ready taproom philosophy. But today it's Buzzcocks' 'Spiral Scratch' because it invented the punk rock independent and, by extension, the underground – taking punk away from the capital elite and giving it to the rest of the country, changing everything in a million ways that it didn't even set out to do.

Before punk, the idea of releasing your own record was utterly alien – after 'Spiral Scratch' it seemed obvious. When I was Growing up in Blackpool, rock stars seemed like they came from Mars – David Bowie actually did come from outer space. So when someone rushed breathlessly into school with a copy of 'Spiral Scratch' in a sleeve that really did look like one of the band had glued it together because, well, they had glued it together, it seemed the most marvellous thing ever. Because the idea that you could make your own record was revolutionary.

On first listen none of this mattered – there was

also the thrill of the rudimentary riffing that somehow still managed to spit out a pop song. There was also that two-, maybe, at a push, three-note guitar solo on 'Boredom'. Three notes is enough for a guitar solo, maybe that should be the law – all guitar players must play three notes and then LEAVE IT.

Pete Shelley managed to make a whole statement in those three notes – a guitar solo that was sarcastic, droll and very, very funny. And we haven't even got to the lyrics yet.

Frontman Howard Devoto had a voice that could out-sneer Johnny Rotten. And he sneered with a northern accent, which was even better. His high-IQ acid-wit lyrics were hilarious and spiteful and made a stark point with every line. Devoto's spiky doggerel on these four songs was so original that they reinvented rock lyric writing – after him came The Fall and Morrissey and a whole host of very northern punk poets, doing that same trick of making the normal seem so surreal and showing us all the inherent ugliness or banality and insecurities of life with a twisted, dark humour.

'I'm standing in the post office buying sticky pictures of the Queen,' he drolled and this really camp backing vocal from Shelley went, 'Stick up'. Perfect!

Buzzcocks were already a key band in the new punk lineage when they made this record. Punk had been around for a few weeks and they were one of the main bands – things were moving fast and legends were getting created at the drop of a hat.

Their story is perhaps the coolest one in punk. They had formed far away from the London punk elite. Messing around at college in Leigh trying to find some sort of direction, Shelley and Devoto, two out-of-step Stooges fans, had read the first ever review of the Sex

Pistols in the *NME*: the one where Steve Jones says he's only into the chaos and not the music. Nowadays every indie band says that after one can of Stella, but then no one said things like that, and they were also telling the truth. Chaos for an indie band in 2009 is arguing with the accountant. The Pistols were instantly fascinating to the two or three freaks in each town in the UK who were feeling around for some sort of incendiary direction.

The coolest thing about Shelley and Devoto, though, is that after reading the review and getting curious about this Sex Pistols band, they borrowed a car and drove down to London from Bolton that very weekend to go and find the Pistols, naively thinking they'd just happen to be playing there.

Oddly enough their hunch proved to be correct and after a quick phone call to the *NME* office they were directed to Malcolm McLaren's shop, Sex where they were told that the Pistols were playing in Wycombe that night and would they be interested in putting the Pistols on in Manchester? They said yeah, even though they had never put a gig on in their lives. At that very moment, that very second, punk rock DIY was invented and a generation was about to be sucked into Xerox, cheap guitars and Sellotape action.

The Pistols gig in Wycombe was a revelation, and the band's sneering attitude and small freaky crew of fans was a thrill for Shelley and Devoto. They taped the gig so they had a template for just what this punk rock stuff was actually about and returned to Manchester with a headful of ideas and a name for their band, after reading a *Rock Follies* article in *Time Out* with the word 'Buzzcocks' in the title. The feature also had the phrase 'Time's Up' in it, which was going to come in handy for a song title for the 'Spiral Scratch' EP.

Brilliant local artist and friend of the band Linder Sterling (who later on designed the iconic sleeve for Buzzcocks' 'Orgasm Addict' single and eventually Devoto's next band Magazine's first album cover) helped them to realise their punk rock look, cutting Howard's hair and adapting his clothes.

Howard Devoto rang around town using the phone numbers from the gig list he compiled for the *New Manchester Review*. He got the Lesser Free Trade Hall for thirty quid – an apt choice of venue for a revolutionary punk rock show, with its background in free-trade radicalism and where the suffragette movement had started.

Buzzcocks couldn't get it together to play at the Sex Pistols gig in Manchester but they went down in local folklore forever for promoting the key punk rock show that changed everything. After the gig, things would never be the same again. Manchester was reinvented that night, Peter Hook went straight out and bought a thirty-quid bass the next day, bands were formed, people's lives were changed.

Buzzcocks changed pop culture with one DIY gig. They took punk rock from the London hipsters and gave it to Manchester and, by extension, the rest of the world. Four weeks later they brought the Pistols back and finally got it together to play themselves at the show. Scratchy film exists of their set. Devoto looks amazing, a skinny beatnik punk rock alien, wired and intense; Pete Shelley looks skinny, young and cool. On bass was Steve Diggle, who had been walking past the Lesser Free Trade Hall the night of the first gig on the way to a meeting, discussing forming a new band with someone else. Malcolm McLaren, who was standing outside the venue, saw him walk past and thought he was the Buzzcocks' bass player – four weeks later he was.

They would play another ten odd gigs with this line-up before recording a demo of a potential album, which has never been released, and the four classic tracks for the 'Spiral Scratch' EP, which they released with a loan of a few hundred quid from Pete Shelley's dad. The day after they released the EP, Devoto left the band, already tired of the restrictions of punk rock. The year of punk, 1977, was barely a week old and one of the movement's key figureheads had bailed out – how cool is that?

He re-emerged with Magazine and invented post-punk, whilst Pete Shelley took over the vocals and turned Buzzcocks into one of the greatest pop bands ever in the UK.

'Spiral Scratch' was one of the key releases in punk. Its four spiky, hip songs, with rough and ready production, invented DIY and indie and showed every just-formed punk band how to release their own records. It's for this reason that I've made it the key punk rock release.

That afternoon, huddled round a crappy stereo in Blackpool, we were enthralled by the daring and deceptive simplicity of the record and we were excited by its northernness.

I knew when I heard 'Spiral Scratch' that I was going to make records of my own.

And so did thousands of other musicians up and down the country, and that's what makes the single so revolutionary.

Contributors

LANE ASHFELDT has had short fiction published in anthologies, writing journals and online literary spaces and has won several awards. www.ashfeldt.com

LAURA BARTON is a feature writer and music columnist for the *Guardian*, and a contributor to *Q, The Word,* and numerous other publications. Her first novel, *The Distillers*, will be published by Quercus in spring 2010. Raised in Lancashire, she now lives in London.

BILLY BRAGG burst onto the music scene in 1983 singing 'I don't want to change the world, I'm not looking for a New England' and has spent 25 years doing the exact opposite. He has recorded a dozen albums and is the author of *The Progressive Patriot: A Search For Belonging*.

JANINE BULLMAN is the editor of *Punk Fiction*, she lives in London with her husband (see below) and cat. She contributes to *Mojo, Record Collector* and *Loud & Quiet* and has had fiction published in a variety of literary journals. She believes in peace, Gene Vincent and men in sharp suits.

LEE BULLMAN is the author of *Blowback*, published by Pan Macmillan in Spring 2009; he lives in London with his wife, elderly cat, and a collection of sensationalist pulp paperbacks. He believes in the freedom of speech, The Coventry Specials, and women who wear garters. Amen.

BILLY CHILDISH was born in 1959 in Chatham, Kent and left school at sixteen. After working in Chatham Naval Dockyard as an apprentice stone-mason, he went on to study painting, which proved unsatisfactory. Billy was diagnosed as dyslexic at the age of 28. Despite this, he has published more than thirty poetry collections and three novels. He has recorded over a hundred albums and exhibited paintings all over the world.

JAY CLIFTON is co-founder and director of Tight Lip live literary events in Brighton. He is the freelance deviser and curator of ScreenTalk events for Barbican Cinema, London. He has written stories and articles for the magazines *Nude*, *Vertigo*, *Little White Lies* and *Seconds*.

ALAN DONOHOE is the lead singer of The Rakes, whose albums include *Capture/Release* and *Ten New Messages*. He has appeared in the *NME*'s annual cool list twice and is either a graduate of biology or physics (reports vary) and a vegan. He writes lyrics on his mobile phone, saving them in a folder named 'My Lyrics'. He is also known for his dance moves, which he says are inspired by Michael Barrymore. The Rakes release a new album *Klang!* in April 2009.

MAX DÉCHARNÉ was born in England, and can still speak English when his business demands it. During the past eighteen years he has flung six books and numerous records at the public – firstly as a member of Gallon Drunk, then since 1995 as the singer with The Flaming Stars. His most recent book is *King's Road – The Rise & Fall of the Hippest Street in the World*, and his next will be published by Serpent's Tail in 2010. www.myspace.com/maxdecharne and www.myspace.com/theflamingstars

JOOLZ DENBY has been a wild card on the literary scene for 25 years now, treading a line from spine-chilling performance-poet to Orange Prize-nominated novelist. She remains an endearingly forthright figure, taking stories from life's darkest corners and lacing them with humour and the hint of better times to come. *Apples & Snakes 2008*, a new album of spoken-word set to music by Justin Sullivan, is now available at www.newmodelarmy.org.

MARTIN LLOYD EDWARDS once discussed modern poetry with someone called Rod live on Radio One with a listening audience of six million. Redbeck Press subsequently published his *Coconut Heart* ('tough, stubborn, intelligent, like knives') which achieved a position of 1,783,000th in the Amazon sales lists (and climbing). He has published poems and stories in many places including *London Magazine, Stand* and The *Red Wheelbarrow*.

LAURA OLDFIELD FORD is an artist and writer living and working in East London. She has been producing her zine *Savage Messiah* since 2005, which incorporates her drawings, writing and montages about psychogeographic drifts around London. www.savagemessiah.com

DAVID GAFFNEY is the author of two collections of short stories – *Sawn off Tales* and *Aromabingo*. His new novel, *Never Never*, is out now. He lives in Manchester. www.davidgaffney.co.uk.

SALENA GODDEN appears in publications including *Drawbridge*, The *Illustrated Ape*, *Nude* magazine, *Salzburg Review*, *Trespass*, *Gay Times* and *Le Gun*. Her fiction and poetry has also been published in many anthologies including Penguin's *IC3*, Canongate's *Fire People*, Serpent's Tail's *Croatian Nights* and Hodder & Stoughton's *Oral*. Her debut childhood memoir *Springfield Road* is to be published in April 2009 through HarperCollins/Harper Press. She is also the lyricist and lead singer in SaltPeter.

FERRY GOUW was born in Indonesia and has been residing in London for the past twelve years. He is an illustrator, designer, director and musician. Having graduated from Central St Martins, where he gained his BA in Art and Design, he took up an MA in Filmmaking at London Film School. He has released two albums with Semifinalists and lives with his girlfriend and baby kitten.

WILL HODGKINSON is the author of *The Ballad Of Britain* (Portico, 2009), a travelogue on British music and folklore, and *Guitar Man* and *Song Man* (Bloomsbury). He writes for the *Guardian*, *The Times*, *Mojo* and *Vogue*, lives in London and has curly hair.

NICHOLAS HOGG was the inaugural winner of the New Writing Ventures Prize for fiction. In 2008 Canongate published his debut novel, *Show Me the Sky*. He has also had work broadcast by BBC Radio 3 and 4, and was twice short-listed for the Eric Gregory Award for young poets. www.nicholashogg.com

STEWART HOME was born in South London in 1962. He is the author of *69 Things To Do With A Dead Princess*, *Tainted Love* and many other books. After dabbling in rock journalism and music, he switched his attention to the art and publishing worlds in the early 80s. www.stewarthomesociety.org

DEV HYNES is a musician/comic book artist who was raised in London, but currently lives in New York. He has played music as various incarnations such as Lightspeed Champion, Test Icicles, N.B as well as playing for many bands.

KATE JACKSON is a singer, songwriter and artist. From 2003 to 2008 she was the lead singer in Sheffield based indie pop band The Long Blondes. She is currently writing her first solo album.

EDWARD LARRIKIN is a musician, performer and writer. Under the guise The Pan I Am, his new record 'Desertland' will be available in 2009. His monologue 'Camusflage Krokodial' was performed at various literary festivals last year, including The London Word festival and the Laugharne Weekend. He lives in a flat by the River Thames and places a hex on the producers of the *X Factor*.

LYDIA LUNCH uses words, music, photography and film as assaultive weapons against authoritarian abuse. Since 1977 she has screamed, kicked, clawed, whispered, shrieked, and generally acted as Greek Fury in the hope that those who need to hear a passionate voice in their darkest hour will find comfort in her battle cry.
www.lydialunch.org and www.myspace.com/lydialunch

JOHNNY MARR is a musician born in Manchester, best known for his role in one of the UK's most influential bands of all time, The Smiths. He went on to form Electronic with New Order's Bernard Sumner and has worked with The Pretenders, The The, Modest Mouse, Johnny Marr & The Healers. He is now a member of The Cribs.

ALISON MOSSHART is one half of The Kills. The American-born singer lives in London. They have so far released three critically acclaimed albums.

KRISSI MURISON is deputy editor at *NME* in London although hopefully, by the time you read this, her visa will have come through and she'll be living in New York and working as music director for *NYLON*.

JOHN NIVEN is a novelist and journalist whose work has appeared in *Esquire*, *Arena*, *Word* and the *Sunday Times*. His latest novel *The Amateurs* is published in spring 2009 by William Heinemann.

KELE OKEREKE is the vocalist and lead guitarist for the band Bloc Party, whose albums include *Silent Alarm*, *A Weekend In The City* and *Intimacy*. He studied English at King's College London. He is currently obsessed with Beyonce Knowles, cupcakes from EAT, and the Real Housewives of Atlanta. He currently lives in Shoreditch, East London with his two cats Kid and Play.

KATE PULLINGER is a writer who works both in print and online. Her new novel, *The Mistress of Nothing*, will be published by Serpent's Tail in 2009. You can find her digital works, including *Inanimate Alice* and *Flight Paths,* at www.katepullinger.com

JOHN ROBB is a punk rock mob orator fiend and a discordant music machine who writes books, tears up stages with Goldblade and zigzags across the TV. 1977 changed his life and his trousers and he celebrates that to this day whilst still being impatient for the new.

PAUL SMITH, born in 1979, is a songwriter from the northeast of England who is best-known as the singer of Maximo Park. The band's first album, *A Certain Trigger*, was released in 2005 and was nominated for the Mercury Music Prize. Two years later, *Our Earthly Pleasures* was released, reaching Number 2 in the UK Charts. His lyrics tend to describe the romance of the everyday and it is with this in mind that he has written his first short story.

CATHI UNSWORTH is the author of *The Not Knowing*, *The Singer* and the editor of the award-winning crime fiction compendium *London Noir*. She began her writing career on *Sounds* in 1987 and still tries to live her life by those great punk DIY ideals. Her new novel *Bad Penny Blues* will be published, like all the others, by Serpent's Tail. www.cathiunsworth.co.uk

PETER WILD is the co-author of *Before the Rain*, a short story collection from Flax Books, and the editor of *The Flash* (an anthology of flash fiction published by Social Disease), *Perverted by Language: Fiction inspired by The Fall* (published by Serpent's Tail) and *The Empty Page: Fiction inspired by Sonic Youth* (published by Serpent's Tail in the UK and, as *Noise: Fiction inspired by Sonic Youth*, in the US by Harper Perennial). His journalism has appeared in the *Guardian, Independent, Time Out, Big Issue* and *Pen Pusher*, amongst others, while his fiction has appeared in numerous journals, e-zines, anthologies and magazines on both sides of the Atlantic, including *Dogmatika, 3AM Magazine, NOO Journal, SN Review, Word Riot, Straight from the Fridge, Thieves Jargon, Pindeldyboz, Scarecrow, The Beat, Litro* and *Lamport Court*.

LOIS WILSON is a vegetarian, socialist, CND supporter and devotee to 60s girl groups and 60s soul. She is also a DJ, author and avid record collector. Before joining *Mojo* in 1999 she lectured in Philosophy and Social Science and worked behind the counter of a record shop. The deputy editor of the late *Mojo Collections*, she has also compiled Universal's Chess reissue series and titles on Trojan, Motown and from Paul Weller's back catalogue.

Thanks to . . .

the best agent you could ever hope to meet, Isabel Atherton at Creative Authors, the legal beagle James Duffett-Smith, my husband Lee Francis Bullman, MWC, George Chen, Jean and Derek Warren, Chris and Dave Howson, Linder Sterling, Terry Edwards, Jeff Barrett, Jodie Banaszkiewicz, Amy Morgan, Joanne Harvey, Julie Hamper, Ian at Damaged Goods, Tina and Rob Partridge, Jello Biafra and John Greenway of the Dead Kennedys, Tony Linkin, Jo Feldman, Liam, Carl, Steve, Helen and everyone at Coalition, Sue Thomas, Claudia Cragg, Joe Moss, Johnny Marr, John Earls, Abigail Wilson, Jo Perfect, Heathcliffe Bird, Toni Lebsuque, Lovely Alice, Lauren Doss, Craig Template, Natalie Castro, Zachery McKraken, Lora Avedian, Janet Choudry, Grace Maxwell, Alexandra Poppoff, Susan Smith at MBA, Jon Savage, Tom Bromley, Malcolm Croft, Katie Cowan, Helen Barnes, Jon Harrington, Bee Lavender, Joe Stretch, Des Murphy, Alice Watts, Lucy Jackson, Niamh Paul and all at Teenage Cancer Trust.

Dedicated to Lee Francis Bullman with love and squalor